云南旅游文化

（汉英对照）

主　编　王晓梅　李　雪　田晓燕
副主编　王　萍　刘芳芳

西南交通大学出版社
·成都·

图书在版编目（CIP）数据

云南旅游文化 = Yunnan Tourism Cultures：汉英对照 / 王晓梅，李雪，田晓燕主编. —成都：西南交通大学出版社，2023.3
ISBN 978-7-5643-9223-9

Ⅰ.①云… Ⅱ.①王… ②李… ③田… Ⅲ.①旅游文化–云南–双语教学–教材–汉、英 Ⅳ.①F592.774

中国国家版本馆 CIP 数据核字（2023）第 052750 号

Yunnan Tourism Cultures
云南旅游文化
Yunnan Lǚyou Wenhua

主编　王晓梅　李　雪　田晓燕

责 任 编 辑	孟　媛
封 面 设 计	墨创文化
出 版 发 行	西南交通大学出版社
	（四川省成都市金牛区二环路北一段 111 号
	西南交通大学创新大厦 21 楼）
发行部电话	028-87600564　028-87600533
邮 政 编 码	610031
网　　　址	http://www.xnjdcbs.com
印　　　刷	四川森林印务有限责任公司
成 品 尺 寸	170 mm × 230 mm
印　　　张	13
字　　　数	207 千
版　　　次	2023 年 3 月第 1 版
印　　　次	2023 年 3 月第 1 次
书　　　号	ISBN 978-7-5643-9223-9
定　　　价	32.00 元

课件咨询电话：028-81435775
图书如有印装质量问题　本社负责退换
版权所有　盗版必究　举报电话：028-87600562

前言 PREFACE

  本教材是校级一流课程——"大学英语（一）"（项目编号：YLKC202105）的主要建设成果，此项目目前已完成建设并结题。项目组的五位成员同时是本教材的参编人员，均是丽江文化旅游学院的一线英语教师。

  英语语言学习不仅是关乎认知与思维的知识与能力的习得过程，更是对语言所承载的文化的领悟与传播过程。云南这片"旅游天堂"蕴含着丰富的文化底蕴，值得挖掘、讲述与传播。

  丽江文化旅游学院三分之二的学生来自云南，基于这一特殊生情，本教辅用书选取云南具有代表性的五个地方：昆明、丽江、大理、西双版纳、香格里拉，作为重点篇章，总计五章，从自然景观、人文内涵（包括人文景观、地方名人）、地方特色（包括美食、手工技艺、建筑、人民生活等）方面呈现彩云之南旅游文化新内涵；同时选取相对有影响力的千年古城建水、水乡玉溪、山水田城弥勒、茶乡普洱与侨乡腾冲，作为其他篇章，通过呈现这五个地方的细微亮点，进一步挖掘云南旅游承载的深厚文化底蕴，呈现云南旅游文化新内涵。

本书突破简单的介绍，在内容选择与语言表达方面注重深度体现云南旅游文化新韵。为提升本书学习效果，每一节内容后面设置"思考并讨论"（Think and Discuss）环节，与相关社会热点、学生生活焦点结合，实现导问引思。

　　作为校级英语教学教辅材料，本书采用中英两种语言编写，旨在带给学习者学英语、品云南的有趣学习"新旅"，重燃英语学习热情，增强英语学习自信心，培养中英思维转换的敏感度，将学生的英语学习提升到一个新高度。本书编者旨在鼓励并希冀学生用所学外语（英语）讲好家乡的故事，传播家乡的旅游文化新蕴。

 引言
Introduction

 第一章　昆明篇
Chapter I　Kunming

004　第一节　四季如春昆明城
　　　Section One　Spring City—Kunming

007　第二节　久远悠长昆明史
　　　Section Two　The Long History of Kunming

012　第三节　记忆满满昆明街
　　　Section Three　Streets Full of Memories in Kunming

016　第四节　地方特色昆明节
　　　Section Four　Festivals with Local Color

021　第五节　功绩卓越昆明路
　　　Section Five　Contributive Kunming Roads

026　第六节　争奇斗艳昆明花
　　　Section Six　Beautiful Kunming Flowers

030　第七节　特色经典昆明味
　　　Section Seven　Kunming Cuisine with Classic Features

037　第八节　深入人心昆明名片
　　　Section Eight　Popular Name Cards of Kunming

044 第九节　英勇无畏昆明英雄
　　　　Section Nine　Brave and Fearless Heroes of Kunming

第二章　丽江篇
Chapter II　Lijiang

050 第一节　只此青绿，看一山一谷
　　　　Section One　The Beautiful Scenery of Yulong Snow Mountain and Blue Moon Valley

052 第二节　"中国桥"飞跃金沙江
　　　　Section Two　The Chinese Bridges Spanning over Jinsha River

055 第三节　智慧古城　民居智慧
　　　　Section Three　The Wisdom in Lijiang Ancient Town and Its Folk Buildings

059 第四节　舌尖记忆　品老味道
　　　　Section Four　The Memory on the Tip of Tongue—The Unforgettable Taste

063 第五节　古乐之韵　音乐活化石
　　　　Section Five　The Living Music Fossil—Naxi Ancient Music

066 第六节　妙手匠心　剪出精彩
　　　　Section Six　The Art of Paper-Cutting

068 第七节　丽江金沙陶　指尖记忆
　　　　Section Seven　Lijiang Jinsha Pottery-Making: Handmade Memory

070 第八节　以赛化友　古朴纯美
　　　　Section Eight　The Local Unique Get-Together—Huacong

第三章　大理篇
Chapter III　Dali

076 第一节　史海寻踪　古迹大理
　　　　Section One　A Wealth of Historical Sites

082　第二节　异彩纷呈　文艺大理
　　　Section Two　Brilliant Folk Arts

087　第三节　文献名邦　人文大理
　　　Section Three　A Prestigious State of Literature and Art

093　第四节　精雕细琢　匠心大理
　　　Section Four　Exquisite Craftsmanship

098　第五节　品茗论道　茶艺大理
　　　Section Five　The Three-Course Tea Ceremony

100　第六节　古朴民居　乡愁大理
　　　Section Six　Traditional Folk Architecture

103　第七节　苍洱摇篮　宜居大理
　　　Section Seven　An Ecologically Livable City

第四章　西双版纳篇
Chapter Ⅳ　Xishuangbanna

107　第一节　勐巴拉娜西，理想而神奇的乐土
　　　Section One　Mengbalanaxi, an Ideal and Magical Paradise

110　第二节　幸福在哪里？西双版纳告诉你
　　　Section Two　Where Is Happiness? You Can Find it in
　　　　　　　　　　Xishuangbanna

120　第三节　物华天宝　人杰地灵
　　　Section Three　Natural Treasures and Outstanding People

132　第四节　树木丛生　百草丰茂
　　　Section Four　Luxuriant Plants

139　第五节　孔雀南飞此处栖，象群河谷自由行
　　　Section Five　Peacocks Flying South and Perching Here,
　　　　　　　　　　Elephants Traveling Freely in the Valley

144　第六节　巧夺天工　匠心独具
　　　Section Six　Superb Workmanship and Unique Ingenuity

146　第七节　相知无远近　万里尚为邻
　　　Section Seven　Though Bosom Friends Miles Apart, No Distance If Sharing a Heart

第五章　香格里拉篇
Chapter V　Shangri-La

148　第一节　人间胜景　香格里拉
　　　Section One　Shangri-La—the Fairyland on Earth

154　第二节　高原的馈赠　享美食之旅
　　　Section Two　Food Culture—Gifts from the Plateau

161　第三节　诗情画意　纳帕海湿地
　　　Section Three　Poetic Painting—Napahai Wetland

164　第四节　奇秀悦目　普达措公园
　　　Section Four　Picturesque Scene—Pudacuo National Park

169　第五节　鸟兽乐园　香格里拉
　　　Section Five　Paradise for Birds and Animals—Shangri-La

174　第六节　创艺之美　香格里拉
　　　Section Six　The Beauty of Crafts

第六章　其他篇
Chapter VI　Charming Places In Yunnan

183　第一节　千年古城建水
　　　Section One　The Thousand-Year Ancient Town—Jianshui County

185　第二节　水乡玉溪
　　　Section Two　Yuxi—a Water City

188　第三节　山水田城弥勒
　　　Section Three　Mile—a Park-Like City

190　第四节　茶乡普洱
　　　Section Four　The Tea Town—Pu'er

193　第五节　侨乡腾冲
　　　Section Five　Tengchon—the Hometown of Overseas Chinese
　　　　　　　　　　and Their Relatives

参考文献
References

引言
Introduction

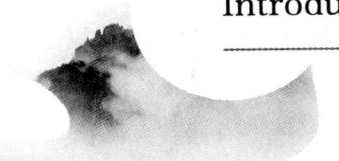

云南,地处祖国大西南,与东南亚多国接壤。这片39.4万平方千米的红土地是中国最多彩的省份,梅里雪山、碧罗雪山、白马雪山、哈巴雪山、玉龙雪山等高冷雪峰林立;滇池、泸沽湖、抚仙湖、洱海等静谧旖旎的高原湖泊点缀于滇中红色高原(包括云南四个城市:昆明、曲靖、楚雄、玉溪);万千水流汇聚成大江大河:独龙江、怒江、澜沧江、金沙江、元江、南盘江,六大江河奔流而下,其势不可阻挡;江河在群山之间劈削出以虎跳峡为代表的中国最为壮观的高山峡谷群,由南并流的金沙江以V字形急转弯成为孕育中华文明的母亲河,堪称万里长江第一湾。较小尺度的立体化塑造也同样精彩:被降水溶蚀而成的石林如同陶渊明笔下的桃花源的溶洞,被降水冲刷成的高大土林,等等。

云南,拥有立体的地理环境和立体的多样气候。南北900余千米的范围内,出现了7个气候带,相当于从海南岛到黑龙江的气候变化。丰富的气候类型孕育了生物的多样性,为生灵的繁衍提供了更多可能性,也成就了云南作为中国"植物王国"的美名,拥有高等植物1.8万多种,占全国一半以上。同时,云南还是中国的"动物王国",兽类、鸟类、鱼类都占到全国种数的50%以上。

云南,宛如一个"孕育所",一共孕育、滋养了26个民族,成为中华民族56个成员中26个的世居家园,也是中国少数民族种类最多的省。多种语言、多样的节日、各式各样的民居、不同的生产方式、多样的美食共同构成了云南五彩缤纷、神奇瑰丽、融合共存的风情与文化。

　　从山川到江河，从动物到植物，从文化到产业，多样的元素集中于此，多元的文化诞生于此，创造了多彩的云南。

　　汇聚万千色彩的彩云之南超乎你的想象，也等待着你的亲临与探索。

　　Yunnan, a province located in the southwest, China, adjoining many countries in Southeast Asia. The red land area of 394,000 square metres has the most varied topography in China. On this land tower aloft many snow mountains including Meili Snow Mountain, Biluo Snow Mountain, Baima Snow Mountain, Haba Snow Mountain, and Yulong Snow Mountain. Charming plateau lakes like Dianchi Lake, Lugu Lake, Fuxian Lake and Erhai Lake beautify the red plateau land—The Central Yunnan Region (including four cities in Yunnan: Kunming, Qujing, Chuxiong and Yuxi). Thousands of big and small lakes and streams converge into six rivers including Dulong River, Nu River, Lancang River, Jinsha River, Yuan River and Nanpan River that run down in a grandeur way, creating the most magnificent high mountain canyon groups represented by Tiger Leap Gorge. The Jinsha River in cocurrent flow in the south takes a sharp turn in the shape of V, becoming the cradle of Chinese civilization, and this is the well-known First Bay of Yangtze River. The multi-dimensional shaping in small scale is also wonderful, like the limestone formed by rainfall erosion, which is much like the karst cave in the Peach Blossom Garden described by Tao Yuanming, and the amazing landscape—Soil Hills formed by rainfall erosion.

　　Yunnan has the multi-dimensional geographical environment and various climates. There are seven climate zones within 900 km from the south to the north, equivalent to the climate change from Hainan island to Heilongjiang, northeast, China. Various climates breed biodiversity and make it more possible for the reproduction of living creatures, which wins Yunnan the prestige of "The Kingdom of Plants" in China with more than 18,000 kinds of advanced plants that accounts for half of the total number nationwide. Yunnan is also known as "The Kingdom of Animals" in China with various beasts, birds and fish accounting for over 50% of the total nationwide.

Yunnan, being a "cradle of ethnic minorities", has nourished 26 ethnic groups, becoming the permanent home to these 26 minorities out of the total 56 in China, and thus becomes the province owning the most minorities in China. Various languages, festivals and delicious foods and different dwelling houses as well as production styles create rich, colorful, magical, and harmoniously co-existential romances and cultures.

From mountains to rivers, from animals to plants, from cultures to industries, Yunnan, where various elements and cultures come together for a colorful life, is such an unprecedented province in China.

Yunnan, a mysterious land gathering various and colorful elements, waiting for you to pay a visit and rediscover its uniqueness that will be beyond your expectation and imagination.

第一章 昆明篇
Chapter I Kunming

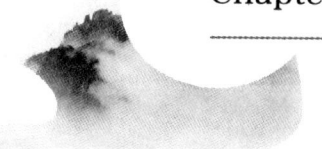

第一节 四季如春昆明城

昆明,别称春城,云南省省会,虽地处中国西南偏远之地,却名扬海内外,每年吸引着数百万人前往。昆明是滇中城市群中心城市,也是国务院批复确定的中国西部地区重要的中心城市之一。截至2022年,全市下辖7个区、6个县、代管1个县级市和3个自治县,总面积21 012.54平方千米。根据第七次人口普查数据,截至2020年11月1日零时,昆明市常住人口为846万人。

昆明地处中国西南地区、云贵高原中部,具有"东连黔桂通沿海,北经川渝进中原,南下越老达泰柬,西接缅甸连印巴"的独特区位优势,处在南北国际大通道和第三座东西向亚欧大陆桥的交汇点。

昆明是国家历史文化名城,早在三万年前就有人类在滇池周围生息繁衍;公元前278年滇国建立,定都于此;公元765年南诏国筑拓东城,为昆明建城之始;明末时期,南明永历政权在昆明建都。

昆明属北亚热带低纬度高原山地季风气候,为山原地貌,三面环山,南濒滇池。由于地处低纬高原而形成"四季如春"的气候,享有"春城"的美誉。

中国昆明进出口商品交易会、中国国际旅游交易会、中国昆明国际旅游节使昆明成为中国主要的会展城市之一。昆明在2018中国大陆最佳商业城市中排名第 23，并被重新确认为国家卫生城市。2019 年 12 月，国家民委授予昆明市"全国民族团结进步示范市"的荣誉称号。

Section One Spring City—Kunming

Though located in the remote area of Southwest China, Kunming is actually world-renowned and attracting millions of visitors every year. Kunming, nicknamed Spring City, is the provincial capital of Yunnan, and the key city in the west part of China approved by the State Council. By 2019, areas under its administration include 7 districts, 6 counties, 1 county-level city as well as 6 autonomous counties, amounting to 21,012.54 square kilometers. According to the seventh population census carried out in Nov. 2020, there are 8,460 thousand residents living here permanently.

Kunming is located in Southwest China and in the middle of Yunnan-Guizhou Plateau. It has the unique location of "connecting the coastal areas through Guizhou and Guangxi in the east, entering Central China via Sichuan and Chongqing in the north, reaching Vietnam, Laos, Thailand and Cambodia in the south, and exchanging with Myanmar, India and Pakistan in the west". Situated at the intersection of the north-south international corridor and the third east-west Eurasian land bridge, it is also a gateway city for China to open to Southeast Asia and South Asia.

Kunming is a famous National Historical and Cultural City. As early as 30,000 years ago, people lived and multiplied around Dianchi Lake. In 278 BC, the Kingdom of Dian was established and its capital was set here. In 765, Nanzhao State built Tuodong City, which was the beginning of Kunming. At the end of the Ming Dynasty, the Yongli regime established its capital in Kunming.

Kunming enjoys a mountainous monsoon climate and a mountain landscape. It is surrounded by mountains on three sides and faces Dianchi Lake in the south. Because of its location on the low latitude plateau, it has a "springlike climate all year round" and enjoys the reputation of "Spring City".

Kunming China Import and Export Fair, China International Travel Mart and Kunming China International Tourism Festival make Kunming one of the major exhibition cities in China. It ranked twenty-third in the Best Commercial Cities in Mainland China in 2018, and was reconfirmed the National Health City. In Deceber 2019, the National Ethnic Affairs Commission of the People's Republic of China granted Kunming as "National Demonstration City for Ethnic Unity and Progress".

> **Think and Discuss:**
> 你的理想城市是四季分明的北国之城，还是四季如春的昆明呢？气候是你选择理想城市的影响因素吗？你选择的标准是什么？

第二节 久远悠长昆明史

昆明拥有 2200 多年的建城史,滇池地区拥有 3000 年的文明史。

约 3 万年前,昆明人的祖先就已在这一带过着茹毛饮血、穴居野外的原始生活。4000~7000 年前,滇池一带已有了定居的农业民族,从事"刀耕火种"的原始农业和狩猎、饲养畜禽等多种经营活动,并已能纺纱、织布。滇池地区的稻谷种植至今至少已有约数千年的历史。新石器时代与青铜器时代滇池地区氏族部落林立,以百濮人为主。氐人、羌人等游牧民族由陕西、甘肃、青海、四川一带越过金沙江进入滇池地区以后,与当地濮人融合形成滇族,促进了滇池地区的开发和发展。

公元前 298 年,楚国大将庄蹻率众入滇,建立了"滇国",也带来了楚国和中原地区先进的文化、技术,促进了滇池地区政治、经济的发展。西汉王朝建立后,积极谋求对"西南夷"地区的开发并以滇池地区为中心设置了益州郡,把中央集权的郡县制度推行到了西南边疆,标志着古代云南接受中央王朝直接统治的开始。郡县制度的施行,有力地促进了滇池地区奴隶制社会的解体。汉族移民和中原先进技术、文化的传播,使滇池地区的经济发展达到了一个新的水平。蜀汉诸葛亮平定南中后,任用"大姓"为地方官吏,实行促进民族团结的政策。到梁末隋初,滇池地区已是"户口殷众,金宝富饶""多骏马、犀象、明珠",成为当时西南在经济上较为繁荣和富庶的地区。

唐代中叶,蒙氏势力在洱海地区崛起,建立南诏国,后于昆川置拓东城。拓东城的开辟,为古代昆明的城市发展奠定了基础。

937 年,大理段氏夺取南诏政权,建立大理国,统一了云南,在拓东城的基础上设鄯阐府,释奴隶,免徭役,进一步瓦解南诏的贵族统治,解放了社会生产力，城市规模进一步扩大，繁华的市中心逐渐移至盘龙江以西（今金碧路、三市街）一带。段氏统治者在鄯阐营造宫室园林，兴修水利，到大理国末期，鄯阐城已发展成为滇中一座"商工颇众"的繁华城市。

元朝，赛典赤入滇后，建立云南行中书省，置昆明县，并把行政中心由大理迁到昆明，昆明命名即始于此。自此，昆明正式成为全省政治、经济、文化的中心，也使滇池地区的政治经济有了新的发展。明代，大量移民进入云南，昆明汉族人口首次超过本地土著居民。

明末清初，吴三桂在昆明建立政权，建立皇宫。清朝后期，清朝把昆明辟为商埠，后又修通滇越铁路，使昆明成为一个开放城市。

"重九起义"推翻了清朝在云南的统治。1928年8月1日，成立昆明市政府。抗日战争时期，昆明成为支撑中国抗战的经济、文化、军事重镇之一，成为著名的"民主堡垒"。外地的工厂、学校内迁，大量的资金、设备和人才流入昆明，促进了昆明经济的短暂繁荣。国民党中央和云南地方的官僚资本纷纷在昆明设置和开办工厂企业，如烟厂等相继建立，为昆明的工业发展奠定了基础。

1949年12月9日，卢汉率部在昆明起义，昆明宣告和平解放。

Section Two   The Long History of Kunming

Kunming has a history of more than 2,200 years, and the Dianchi Lake area has 3,000 years of civilization.

About 30,000 years ago, the ancestors of Kunming people had already lived a primitive life in the wild in this area. About 4,000 to 7,000 years ago, there were settled agricultural people in the area of Dianchi Lake, who engaged in primitive agriculture of slash-and-burn farming, hunting, raising livestock, poultry and doing other diversified business activities, and were able to weave yarn and cloth. Rice cultivation in the Dianchi Lake area has a history of at least 7,000 years. In the Neolithic Age and Bronze Age, the area was full of clans and tribes, mainly Baipu people. The Di people, Qiang people and other nomads from Shaanxi, Gansu, Qinghai and Sichuan crossed the Jinsha River and entered the area. They merged with the local Pu people and formed the Dian people, which promoted the development of the area.

In 298 BC, Zhuang Qiao, a general of the State of Chu, led his troops into Yunnan and established the Dian Kingdom, which brought advanced culture and technology from Chu and the central plains, thus promoted the politics and economy of the Dianchi Lake area. After the establishment of the Western Han Dynasty, it actively sought to develop the area of "Southwest Yi" and set up Yizhou County centering on the Dianchi Lake area, which popularized the centralized county system to the southwest frontier, marking the beginning of the ancient Yunnan accepting the direct rule of the central dynasty. The implementation of county system effectively promoted the disintegration of the slavery society in the Dianchi Lake area. Han immigrants and the spread of advanced technology and culture from Central Plains brought the economic development of Dianchi Lake area to a new level. After Zhuge Liang pacified Nanzhong, he appointed Daxing as local officials and implemented the policy of promoting national unity. By the end of the Liang Dynasty and the beginning of the Sui Dynasty, this area had become an economically prosperous area in the southwest at that time.

In the middle of the Tang Dynasty, the Meng's clan rose in Erhai area and established Nanzhao State, which was later settled in Kunchuan in Tuodong City. The opening of Tuodong City laid a foundation for the development of ancient Kunming.

In 937, Dali Duan's clan captured Nanzhao regime, set up Dali Kingdom and unified Yunnan. On the basis of Tuodong City, they set Shanchan Mansion (government office), released slaves, and reduced corvee, leading to the further collapse of Nanzhao aristocracy and the development of social productive forces. The city scale was expanded and the center of downtown gradually moved to the west of Panlong River (now Jinbi Road, Three City Street). Duan's rulers built palaces and gardens as well as water conservancy facilities in Shanchan. By the end of Dali State, Shanchan had developed into a prosperous city with many merchants and workers in central Yunnan.

In the Yuan Dynasty, Saidianchi entered Yunnan, established Yunnan Provincial Government Office, set Kunming County, and moved the administrative center from Dali to Kunming. Kunming was named from this. Since then, Kunming has officially become the political, economic and cultural center of the province. Politics and economy in Dianchi Lake area also had a new development. In the Ming Dynasty, a large number of immigrants entered Yunnan, and the Han population in Kunming surpassed the local population for the first time.

At the end of the Ming Dynasty and the beginning of the Qing Dynasty, Wu Sangui established a government in Kunming and built an imperial palace. In the late Qing Dynasty, Kunming was opened as a commercial port, and then the Yunnan-Vietnam Railway was built, making Kunming an open city.

The Double Ninth Uprising overthrew the Qing Dynasty in Yunnan. On August 1, 1928, Kunming Municipal Government was established. During the War of Resistance Against Japanese Aggression, Kunming became one of the important economic, cultural and military towns supporting China's War of Resistance Against Japanese Aggression, and known as a famous "fortress of democracy". Factories and schools from other places moved in, and a large amount of capital, equipment and talents flowed into Kunming, which promoted the brief prosperity of Kunming's economy. The central committee of the Kuomintang Party and the local bureaucrat capital of Yunnan set up factories and enterprises in Kunming one after another, such as tobacco factories, which laid a foundation for the industrial development of Kunming.

On December 9, 1949, Lu Han led an uprising in Kunming, and Kunming declared peaceful liberation.

> **Think and Discuss:**
> 不同的历史塑造了魅力各异的城市，请查阅、了解你所在城市的历史，透过历史挖掘蕴于生活的历史感并分享。

第三节　记忆满满昆明街

如果说成都有宽窄巷子，上海有新天地，那么昆明就有昆明老街。昆明老街是昆明这座历史文化名城唯一保留下来的一片原汁原味的老街区，是昆明市面积最大、保存清代和民国时期特色民居建筑、商铺建筑最多的片区，具有较高的历史价值、文化价值和情感价值。

昆明老街的历史可追溯到大理国时代，它经历元、明、清多个朝代更迭，一直保存至今。现今尚存的昆明老街的格局，是从清代康熙年间云贵总督在此建署而逐步开始形成的，为昆明老街留下了深深的历史烙印。一批近代建筑和私人豪宅的兴建，又为昆明老街留下了民国时期的历史风貌。然而，无情的时光却让美丽变得斑驳，昆明的"城市之心"也在岁月的侵蚀下变得破败不堪。现在，昆明老街迎来了改造项目，在建设云南旅游文化大省的强劲东风下，保护这个独特的旅游文化资源，为现代旅游文化经济做出贡献。相信昆明的文化历史可以在昆明老街得以全方位的展示，昆明老街又迎来了生命的第二个春天。

昆明老街一直以来都是昆明商业街区中最有活力的部分。近几年来，昆明老街内传统的文化、商贸活动不但没有减少，反而人气更加旺盛，有日益扩大的趋势。

昆明老街光华街，东起正义路，西至五一路，全长435米，是昆明城中仅存的具有昆明古朴风貌的老街。在今天的光华街上，可以吃到口味正宗的小锅米线，可以淘到光怪陆离的云南古玩，可以找到历经百年的药铺。光华街用它斑驳古朴的胸襟包容着昆明的古今。

昆明老街甬道街早在1983年，就有了昆明最早的花鸟市场。随着时间的推移，当年在甬道街上搭建铁皮棚，售卖花鸟鱼虫的商家在赚得盆满钵满之后，纷纷外扩，陆续形成了景星珠宝花鸟市场。此外，这些代表城市市井特色的小买卖甚至延伸到光华街、文明街。如今，甬道街的改造升级完成，那些曾一度外迁的商家带回自己升级后的商品回归。

昆明老街景星街，每日总是人潮汹涌，纷至沓来的本地人或外地游客，或购物，或闲逛。各种稀奇古怪的东西都可以在这里淘到，景星街承载了太多昆明人美好的童年记忆，也为各种外地游客带来无尽的惊喜。

昆明老街钱王街，潮流与历史在此对撞，这里有老宅子中的咖啡馆，有英国专业的电音酒吧，还有很多手工艺人的精品商店，在这里街拍的游客络绎不绝。

Section Three   Streets Full of Memories in Kunming

If there are wide and narrow alleys in Chengdu and Xintiandi in Shanghai, then there are old streets in Kunming. Kunming Old Street is the only original old street preserved in Kunming, a famous historical and cultural city. It is the largest area in Kunming and has the most characteristic residential buildings and shops built in Qing Dynasty and the Republic of China. It has high historical, cultural and emotional value.

The history of Kunming Old Street can be traced back to the time of Dali Kingdom. It went through the changes of dynasties like Yuan, Ming and Qing and has been preserved until now. The existing pattern of Kunming Old Street was gradually formed from the establishment of the office by Governor Yungui during the reign of Kangxi in Qing Dynasty, leaving a deep historical imprint on Kunming Old Street. The construction of a number of modern buildings and private mansions has left the historical style of the Republic of China period for Kunming Old Street. However, the merciless time has made the beauty become mottled, and the "heart of the city" of Kunming has become dilapidated under the erosion of time. Now, Kunming Old Street ushered in the transformation project, that is to protect the unique tourism and cultural resources, and make contributions to the modern tourism and cultural economy with the chance of building Yunnan a tourism and culture province. It is believed that the culture and history of Kunming can be fully displayed in Kunming Old Street, and Kunming Old Street has ushered in the second spring of life.

Kunming Old Street has always been the most dynamic part of Kunming's commercial district. In recent years, the traditional cultural and commercial activities in the old streets of Kunming have not been reduced, but become more popular and have a growing trend of expansion.

Guanghua Street, running from Zhengyi Road in the east to Wuyi Road in the west, with a total length of 435 meters, is the only old street with the ancient style of Kunming. In today's Guanghua Street, you can eat the authentic small pot rice noodles, find strange Yunnan antiques as well as century-old medicine shops. Guanghua Street holds the ancient and modern times of Kunming with his mottled and simple mind.

As early as 1983, there was the earliest Flower and Bird Market in Yongdao Street in Kunming. With the passage of time, those who built tin booths on Yongdao Street and sold flowers, birds, fish and insects had made a lot of money, then expanded one after another and formed Jingxing Jewelry, Flower and Bird Market. In addition, these small businesses representing the characteristics of the city market even extended to Guanghua and Wenming Street. Now the renovation of Yongdao Street has been completed, and the merchants who once moved out of the city have returned with their upgraded goods.

Jingxing Street, an old street in Kunming, is always crowded with locals and tourists, shopping or relaxing. All kinds of strange things can be found here. Jingxing Street carries many beautiful childhood memories of Kunming people, and also brings endless surprises for all tourists.

Qianwang Street, another old street in Kunming, meets the trend and history here. There are coffee shops in the old houses, professional British electric bars, and many boutique shops of craftsmen. Tourists taking pictures on streets are frequently seen here.

Think and Discuss:

老街、老巷、老桥、老路，承载着几代人满满的回忆，也是一段段历史的见证。在城市化的进程中，我们应该如何保护好它们呢？谈谈你的想法。

第四节　地方特色昆明节

昆明各族人民的节庆，除与全国完全相同的，如元旦、劳动节、国庆节等外，其他传统节令，具有强烈的地方特色和民族特点。略叙于下：

正月，春节是一年中最为隆重的节日。各家居民都要挂年画，张贴红纸金字的春联，室内张灯结彩，以示吉庆。除夕之夜，各家张罗年货，都要购一只大米花团，以示全家团圆。不少人家里要购香橼和佛手柑各一只，用以供奉祖先。屋内铺上一层青翠的松毛，全家在青松毛上秉烛旦达，谓之"守岁"。及至年初一，蒸年糕——意为年年高；吃长白菜——意为清白；吃炒饵块芹菜——取意勤勤快快；吃鱼——意为年年有余……这一天基本不出门。从初二起，亲朋好友互相走访拜望，互赠贺礼。长辈给前来拜年的晚辈压岁钱。在公共场所，耍狮舞龙，踩高跷，文艺演出，一般至初五方罢。正月初九，市民多赶金殿庙会，在郁葱的山间自办野炊。正月十五日元宵节，大街小巷张灯结彩，近年则多举行各种灯展。

二月，在公历"三八"妇女节前后，昆明市民几乎倾城出动，争赶圆通山花会。时值风和日丽，鸟语花香之际，圆通山樱花、海棠竞相怒放，云蒸霞蔚，一片绯红。此时山上山下花潮人潮，蔚为大观。

三月三，耍西山，已经成为昆明人民喜爱的春游活动，百年来未曾衰微过。清明前后，居民则合家上坟祭祖，昔时郊外清冷荒凉的山上，一时万人攒动。各单位则组织青少年祭扫烈士墓，缅怀先烈以启迪后人。

五月最重要的是端午节。此时城中各处的农贸市场里，大批糯米、粽子、粽叶上市，市民喜食发豆芽——以蚕豆泡水发芽后煮食，饮雄黄酒，服平散胃。居家门头悬挂菖蒲、艾叶，以避邪驱虫。

七月中元节，俗称七月半，有祭祖之习。从11日开始至15日结束，一些当地人会沿街摆祭供果、焚烧纸钱。圆通寺、华亭寺等佛教寺院举办大规模的盂兰盆会，超度亡人。

八月中秋节，是一年中仅次于春节的隆重节庆。各家购月饼（俗称"四两坨"），以及青豆、板栗、苞谷、藕等物。亲朋好友，习惯互赠礼物。每至夕阳西坠，朗朗明月升起时，合家团聚，或至大观楼、翠湖，或在院内欢聚，共赏明月。近年来多为丰富多彩的集体活动所代替。

九月重阳节，主要标志是购食重阳糕和到近郊登高。由于和国庆节、教师节相近，因而多有集体活动。

冬月，冬至前后，昆明往往晴空万里，阳光和煦。一般人家会利用假日，上坟祭祖。

腊月岁末，各家都有"扫尘"的良好习俗。粉刷墙壁，洗涤衣物被盖锅灶及家具用品，把一年来的沉积污垢作彻底的清理，以崭新清洁的环境来迎接新春的到来。

Section Four Festivals with Local Color

Except for the New Year's Day, the Labor Day and the National Day, the celebration of other traditional festivals of Kunming people has strong local and ethnic characteristics. The brief introductions are as follows:

Spring Festival in the first lunar month is the most important day of the year. All Kunming residents hang New Year pictures, put up Spring Festival couplets with red paper and gold characters, and decorate houses with lanterns and lights to show their hope for good luck. On the eve, each family would buy tons of goods, for example, popped rice which symbolizes the reunion of family members. Many families would like to buy one sweet rafter and one bergamot to worship their ancestors. They would also pave house floor with verdant pine, then the whole family stay up all through the night, which is called "Shousui". On the first day of the New Year, people steam rice cake to express their hope for a better future life; eat long cabbage which means innocence; eat fried rice cake with celery, hoping to be diligent the next year; eat fish which means they would have more than enough money and food in the following years. They do not go out on that day. On the second day, friends and relatives visit each other and give each other gifts. Elders give the younger generation New Year's money. Lion and dragon dance, stepping on the stilts, and other arts performing would be held for the public and usually be ended on the fifth day of the first lunar month. On the ninth day of the first lunar month, citizens gather at the Golden Temple and have picnics on the mountains. Then on the Lantern Festival which falls on the fifteenth day of the first lunar month, people would decorate lanes and streets with colorful lanterns and lights, while in recent years, they prefer to hold a variety of lantern exhibitions.

In February, just around the International Women's Day on March 8, almost all residents of Kunming go out for the Flower Meeting on the Yuantong Mountain. Then the wind is gentle and warm, the sun is bright, birds whisper, and cherry blossoms and begonia of Yuantong Mountain are in full bloom, like pink clouds from a distance, which attract numerous visitors to come.

On the third day of the third lunar month, dancing and singing on the West Hill are the favorite spring tour activities of Kunming people. The tradition has been performed every year over the past hundred years.

In the fourth lunar month, people would celebrate Tomb Sweeping Festival. They mainly go to the tomb to offer sacrifices to their ancestors. Then mountains in the suburbs were crowded with thousands of people. Many units or groups would organize teenagers to visit martyrs' tombs in memory of our revolutionary martyrs and for educating the youths.

The most important day in the fifth lunar month is the Dragon Boat Festival. At that time, a large number of Zongzi, made of glutinous rice and reed leaves are on the market. The public like to eat the boiled bean sprouts, drink realgar wine, which is good for unwinding the stomach. They would hang calamus and artemisia argyi leaves on the door to ward off evil insects.

The seventh lunar month is the time to celebrate Zhongyuan Festival, commonly known as July and a Half. There are rites of worshipping ancestors from the eleventh day to fifteenth day. Some residents would put fruits and burn paper money along the street. In Yuantong Temple, Huating Temple, Buddhas would hold large-scale ceremonies over the dead.

In the eighth lunar month, people celebrate Middle Autumn Day which is a grand one, second only to the Spring Festival. Every family would buy moon cakes (commonly known as "Siliangtuo"), green beans, chestnuts, corns, lotus roots and other things. Relatives and friends would give gifts to each other. In the evening, as moon is rising, the whole family would reunion at home, or go to the Daguan or Cuihu Park to appreciate moon. In recent years, various collective activities are preferred among Kunming people.

On the Double Ninth Day, it is a custom for people to buy cakes and go hill climbing in suburbs. For the day is quite close to the National Day and Teachers' Day, there are usually collective activities.

In the eleventh lunar month, it is usually sunny and warm in Kunming. Ordinary people would visit graves to honor their ancestors on holidays.

At the end of the twelfth lunar month, all the members of the family have the good custom of "sweeping the dust", painting the wall, doing the laundry, cleaning cooking utensils and furniture. They do such a thorough cleaning to welcome the new spring.

> **Think and Discuss:**
> 不同的地域、时空、文化、物产赋予了中国传统节日不同的庆祝方式，你家乡的庆祝方式有哪些特色与不同？

第五节　功绩卓越昆明路

（一）滇越铁路①

"云南十八怪，火车没有汽车快，不通国内通国外"，这句广为流传的民谣很大程度上源于滇越铁路。

滇越铁路是中国最早修筑的铁路之一。它连接了云南省会昆明与越南首都河内和其北方最大港口城市海防。这条国际铁路全长854千米，分南北两大段：南段在越南境内，自海防至中越边境，1901年动工，1903年建成，全长389千米；北段在中国境内，自中越边境经碧色寨、开远、宜良至昆明，全长465千米，于1903年动工，1910年竣工。

由于建设背景和联运需要，滇越铁路采用了东南亚地区普遍使用的1000毫米轨距（俗称米轨），与相连的蒙（自）宝（秀）铁路一起，成为中国大陆唯一的窄轨干线铁路系统。与地形相对平缓的滇越铁路南段不同，滇越铁路云南段80%的路段穿行在险峻的群山之间，筑有桥梁173座，隧道150个"桥隧相连，弯急坡陡"可谓滇越铁路的真实写照，因此工程异常艰巨。纵然在同等条件下米轨铁路的工程量远远小于准轨，但滇越铁路的单位公里建设费用却比当时中国其他地区的准轨铁路高出一倍，全线建设费用更是高达1.58亿法郎，其工程之浩大可见一斑。与此同时，滇越铁路亦采用了当时世界上最先进的设计与技术，代表了当时铁路工程的最高水平，"人字桥"至今仍是工程教科书的典范。被《泰晤士报》称为与巴拿马运河、苏伊士运河并列的"世界三大工程奇迹"。

滇越铁路满足了当时比较落后的滇南地区的经济生活需要，多年来自

---

① 资料来源：滇越铁路——一个法国家庭在中国的经历. 滇越铁路——中国西南地区的第一条铁路. 杨培成. 云南学习平台，"学习强国"平台，2020年11月9日，摘自2021年8月15日。

王家营车站以南，货物运输繁忙，列车运行稠密，以低于公路运输的运费实现了大批货物的流通。这条不堪负载的铁路一直运行到2010年，如今，鉴于滇越铁路在跨国经济文化活动中起到了重要作用，沿途多元文化保存完好，自然风光美丽多样等原因，其遗产价值正在被深入研究。

（二）滇缅公路

滇缅公路，即云南到缅甸的公路，又称抗日公路，起于昆明止于缅甸腊戍，全长1 146千米。滇缅公路于1937年开始修建，历经九个月的艰苦奋斗抢修而成，打破了日军三个月内灭亡中国的妄想。据不完全统计，整个抗日战争期间，通过滇缅公路运进的军用和民用物资达77万余吨，进出汽车1万多辆，被称为"抗战输血管"，从物资上给了抗战巨大的支持。滇缅公路的建成有利于国内工业和对外贸易的发展，为中国抗战的胜利奠定了有力的物资基础。滇缅公路的修筑增强了国人的凝聚力，提高了中国人民坚持抗战的信心和决心，也让世界充分认识到中国人民的伟大力量。

Section Five Contributive Kunming Roads

Yunnan-Vietnam Railway

"Yunnan has 18 strange things. The train can't run as fast as the car, and it can connect not the home but the foreign country." This popular folk song largely originated from the Yunnan-Vietnam railway.

The Yunnan-Vietnam Railway is one of the earliest railways built in China. It links Kunming, with Hanoi, the capital of Vietnam, and Haiphong, its largest port city in the north. This international railway is 854 kilometers long, and can be divided into two major sections: the southern section in Vietnam, from Haiphong to the China-Vietnam border, which was started in

1901 and completed in 1903, with a total length of 389 kilometers; the northern section in China, running 465 kilometers from the China-Vietnam border through Bise Zhai, Kaiyuan and Yiliang to Kunming, which was constructed between 1903 and 1910.

Due to the background of the construction and the need for combined transportation, the Yunnan-Vietnam Railway adopted the 1000mm gauge (commonly known as meter gauge) commonly used in Southeast Asia, and together with the connected Meng-Bao Railway, it became the only narrow gauge trunk railway system in Chinese mainland. Different from the southern section of the Yunnan-Vietnam Railway, which has relatively gentle terrain, 80% of the Yunnan section of the Yunnan-Vietnam Railway runs through steep mountains, with 130 bridges, and 150 tunnels. "The bridges and tunnels are connected, and the curve and slope are very steep" can be described as the true portrayal of the Yunnan-Vietnam Railway, so the project is extremely difficult. Even though the construction amount of meter-gauge railway is far less than that of quasi-gauge railway under the same conditions, the construction cost per kilometer of Yunnan-Vietnam railway is twice higher than that of quasi-gauge railway in other parts of China at that time, and the construction cost of the whole line is as high as 160 million francs. You can see the enormity of the project. At the same time, the Yunnan-Vietnam Railway also adopt the most advanced design and technology in the world at that time, representing the highest level of railway engineering at that time, and the "Herb-shaped bridge" is still a model in engineering textbooks today. The *Times* called it one of the "three engineering wonders of the world" along with the Panama Canal and the Suez Canal.

The Yunnan-Vietnam Railway met the needs of economic life in the south of Yunnan, which was relatively backward at that time. For many years, from the south of Wangjiaying station, there had been busy freight transportation and dense train operation, which realized the circulation of a large number of goods at a freight cost lower than that of road transportation. This heavy railway has been in operation until 2010. Now, due to the important role played by the Yunnan-Vietnam Railway in transnational economic and cultural activities, the well-preserved multi-culture along the way and the beautiful and diverse natural scenery, its heritage value is being studied in depth.

Yunnan-Burma Road

The Yunnan-Burma Road, the road from Yunnan to Burma, also known as the Anti-Japanese Road, starts from Kunming and ends in Lashio, Burma, with a total length of 1,146 kilometers. The construction was started in 1937 and finished in 9 mouths with the greatest effort, thus ruined Japanese troops'delusion of perishing China in 3 months. According to incomplete statistics, over 770,000 tons of military and civilian materials were transported through the Burma Road during the the War of Resistance Against Japanese Aggression, and more than 10,000 vehicles were transported in and out of the road, which was known as the "blood transfusion tube for the War of Resistance Against Japanese Aggression", giving great support to the War of Resistance Against Japanese Aggression in terms of materials. The construction of the Burma Road was beneficial to the development of domestic industry and foreign trade, and laid a strong material foundation for China's victory in the War of Resistance Against Japanese Aggression. The construction of the Burma Road strengthened the cohesion of the Chinese people, raised the confidence and determination of the Chinese people to persevere in the war of resistance, and let the world fully realize the great strength of the Chinese people.

Think and Discuss:

改革开放40多年以来,我国社会发生了天翻地覆的改变,尤其是道路建设,发生了突飞猛进的变化。道路建设是经济发展的必要前提,没有便利的交通,就没有经济的发展,从具体实际出发,谈谈你家乡的道路建设与经济发展。

第六节　争奇斗艳昆明花

昆明斗南花卉市场毗邻昆明市呈贡区滇池东岸，享有"金斗南"之称，现已发展成为亚洲最大的鲜切花交易市场，是著名的花都。昆明斗南花卉市场位于云南省昆明市呈贡区斗南街道，距离老花卉市场只有200米距离，对于鲜切花的采购和市场价格调研十分方便。呈贡区距离昆明市区只有18千米，距离昆明长水国际机场36千米，距南昆货运站仅5千米，交通运输条件方便。

云南省80%以上的鲜切花和周边省份、周边国家的花卉入场交易。在全国80多个大中城市中占据70%的市场份额，出口46个国家和地区。有全国10枝鲜切花7枝产自云南之说。多年来借助"斗南"花卉这一中国驰名商标的品牌效应和市场优势，斗南已成为中国花卉市场的"风向标"和花卉价格的"晴雨表"。

昆明斗南花卉市场连续十几年交易量、现金量、人流量和出口额居全国第一。每天上万人次入场交易，日现金流量1千万元左右，旺季达2千万元。2010年2月引进投资38.87亿元，将昆明斗南花卉市场升级打造成占地1020亩[①]、总建筑面积81万平方米的昆明斗南国际花卉产业园区。昆明斗南国际花卉产业园区建成后，创造了近万个就业岗位，实现年交易额100亿元（远期300亿元），承担国家赋予的"带动全国、影响世界"的历史使命。

昆明斗南花卉市场的繁荣带动了花卉相关产业及旅游业的蓬勃发展，每年到斗南花卉市场参观、旅游的外国游客约3万人，国内游客4万余人，散客10万余人。昆明斗南花卉市场的建成使用，成为云南省农业产业结构

---

① 1亩≈666.7平方米。

调整的一个典范，五年来带动云南省花卉苗木种植户达 10 万余户，面积 20.8 万亩，市场吸纳下岗职工 1500 余人、农村富余劳力 3 000 余人，扩大了再就业渠道，市场的繁荣带动了花卉相关产业的发展，促进了农村小城镇建设。几年来，斗南花卉市场充分发挥了引导示范和辐射带动作用，对云南乃至我国花卉产业的发展壮大、产业结构的优化和农村经济的发展产生了显著的推动作用。

Section Six Beautiful Kunming Flowers

Kunming Dounan Flower Market is adjacent to the east bank of Dianchi Lake, Chenggong District, Kunming City, and enjoys the title of "Golden Dounan". Kunming Dounan Flower Market, now developed into the largest fresh cut flower market in Asia, is a famous capital of flower. It is only 200 meters far from old flower market, so the purchase of cut flowers and market price survey are very convenient to be done. It is only 18 kilometers far from Chenggong district, 36 kilometers from Kunming Changshui International Airport, and only 5 kilometers far to Nankun freight assembly station, thus it enjoys convenient transportation.

More than 80 percent of Yunnan's fresh cut flowers are traded with flowers from neighboring provinces and countries. It occupies 70% market share in more than 80 large and medium-sized cities in China, and exports to 46 countries and regions. It is said that 7 of the 10 fresh cut flowers in China are produced in Yunnan. Over the years, with the help of the brand effect and market advantage of "Dounan" flowers, a well known brand in China, Dounan has become the "weather vane" of China's flower market and the "barometer" of flower price.

Kunming Dounan Flower Market has ranked first in China in terms of transaction volume, cash volume, visitor flow and export volume for more than ten consecutive years. There are more than 10 thousand traders per day. The daily cash flow is about 10 million yuan, up to 20 million yuan in peak seasons. In February 2010, it introduced investment of 3.887 billion yuan to upgrade Kunming Dounan Flower Market into Kunming Dounan International Flower Industrial Park, which covers an area of 1,020 mu① and a total construction area of 810,000 square meters. With the completion of Kunming Dounan International Flower Industrial Park, it created obout 10,000 jobs, realize the annual turnover of 10 billion yuan (30 billion yuan in the future), and undertake the historical mission of "driving the whole country and influencing the world" entrusted by the state.

The prosperity of Kunming Dounan Flower Market has led to the vigorous development of flower related industries and tourism. Every year, there are about 30,000 foreign tourists, 40,000 domestic tourists and more than 100,000 individual tourists visiting and traveling in Dounan Flower Market. The completion and using of flower market in Kunming became a model of agricultural industrial structure adjustment in Yunnan province. In past five years, it had driven more than 100,000 households into flowers nursery stock farmers in Yunnan province, covered an area of 208,000 mu. The market had absorbed more than 1,500 laid-off workers and over 3,000 rural surplus labor, expanded employment channels, and the prosperity of the market had also driven the development of flower industry, promoting the construction of small rural towns. In recent years, Dounan Flower Market has played an important role in guiding, demonstrating and radiating the development of Yunnan and

---

① Mu is a Chinese measurement unit. One mu is about 666.7 square meter.

even our nation's flower industry, the optimization of industrial structure and the development of rural economy.

> **Think and Discuss:**
> 昆明鲜花是美的使者,带着芬芳飞向世界,装点着每一个角落。它也是经济和社会发展的功臣,带领斗南人们奔向了富裕和美好。鲜花于你又有怎样的蕴意与寓意呢?

第七节 特色经典昆明味

（一）陈老燕风味凉卷粉

陈老燕风味凉卷粉是第二批"昆明老字号"。它家的凉卷粉"够味、够真、够放心"，不需要刻意的精心包装与夸大宣传，从其制作流程、精良的选料、不含任何添加剂、祖传秘制酱油、数十种调味料，可以看出其对美食的态度——重德厚信。

（二）过桥米线

过桥米线是云南滇南地区特有的小吃，属滇菜系，起源于蒙自地区，由汤料、佐料、生的里脊肉片、鸡脯肉片、乌鱼片、五成熟的猪腰片、肚头片、水发鱿鱼片制作而成。辅料有豌豆尖、韭菜、芫荽、葱丝、草芽丝、姜丝、玉兰片、豆腐皮。主食是用水略烫过的米线。鹅油封面，汤汁滚烫，但不冒热气。被云南省餐饮与美食行业协会、昆明市餐饮与美食行业协会评为"昆明十大名小吃"之一。

（三）烧饵块

烧饵块是云南当地的一种民俗小吃。用煮熟的大米饭压成块状或圆形薄饼状，在炭火上烤制，然后涂上酱料和菜馅即可。做法与糍粑相同，但糍粑的原料是糯米，饵块的原料是大米。烧饵块的来源：民国期间，玉溪人翟永安在昆明端仕街开设的永顺园，以专卖此品出名。被云南省餐饮与美食行业协会、昆明市餐饮与美食行业协会评为"昆明十大名小吃"之一。

（四）鲜花饼

鲜花饼是以云南特有的食用玫瑰花入料的酥饼，是具有云南特色的经典点心代表。鲜花饼在云南当地的各烘焙品店均有销售。鲜花饼也是中国四大月饼流派滇式月饼的经典代表之一。鲜花饼的制作源于300多年前的清代，由上等玫瑰花制作的鲜花饼，因其特色风味列为宫廷御点，深得乾隆皇帝喜爱。近代滇式鲜花饼以1945年昆明冠生园生产的鲜花饼为起源，当年在昆明的西坝还专门开辟一块地种植食用鲜花用来加工鲜花饼和玫瑰糖。

（五）石林乳饼

驰名中外的石林乳饼以山羊奶为原料精制而成，是云南著名特色食品之一。石林乳饼产于石林县的圭山、西街口等地，是一种高脂肪、高蛋白的食品，营养丰富、味道鲜美、食用方便，可以烹制成各种美味菜肴，加之制作简单、容易保存，深受人们喜爱。乳饼的吃法很多，可蒸、烩、煎、炸或生吃，或做成其他形美色鲜的菜肴。

（六）摩登粑粑

昆明的摩登粑粑起源于老昆明的椒盐饼。据坊间流传：该店有两个摩登女郎用美国黄油来和面，现煎热卖椒盐饼，味道非常可口，颇受顾客青睐。顾客不知这粑粑叫椒盐饼，看卖粑粑的女郎打扮十分摩登，就称之为摩登粑粑，从此在昆明就传叫开来，成为昆明小吃的一个品牌。被云南省餐饮与美食行业协会、昆明市餐饮与美食行业协会评为"昆明十大名小吃"之一。

（七）官渡粑粑

官渡粑粑，出自官渡古镇，是具有云南特色的风味小吃。它是一种面食，烘制而成。粑粑内含芝麻、花生、核桃等磨细的果仁与白糖混合为馅，松软香甜，十分可口。在官渡热闹的集市上，几乎每个人都拿着一个粑粑，像是古镇里一道独特的风景。

（八）都督烧卖

都督烧卖是一道起源于昆明宜良的小吃，属于卤菜。宜良烧卖，何以冠以都督二字？说来有一段趣闻。相传，清宣统年间，宜良城有一祝氏映兴园，专卖煮品、烧卖、卤菜，尤以烧卖出名。云南督军唐继尧亲临此店慕名吃烧卖，此事后被传为佳话，"都督烧卖"由此得名。都督烧卖加盐又不咸，蘸醋又不酸。肉多而不腻，馅多又含汁。被云南省餐饮与美食行业协会、昆明市餐饮与美食行业协会评为"昆明十大名小吃"之一。

（九）宜良烤鸭

宜良烤鸭起源于明朝，已有 600 多年的历史，堪称"滇菜魁首"，其中尤以宜良县的"狗街烤鸭"制作最为考究。烤出的鸭，表皮呈枣红色，脆而不焦，肉质鲜嫩，非常可口。2009 年宜良烤鸭被列入第二批省级非物质文化遗产。

Section Seven Kunming Cuisine with Classic Features

Chen Laoyan Flavor Rolled Cold Noodles

Chen Laoyan flavor rolled cold noodles are the second batch of Kunming Time-honored brands. The rolled cold noodles of Chen family is "tasteful, true and assured", which does not need deliberate careful packaging and exaggerated publicity. From its process, excellent selection of materials, zero additives, ancestral secret soy sauce, and dozens of seasonings, we can see their attitude towards food—attaching great importance to virtue and sincerity.

Crossing the Bridge Rice Noodles

Crossing the bridge rice noodles is a special snack in southern Yunnan Province. It belongs to Yunnan cuisine and originates from Mengzi region. It is made of soup, seasoning, raw tenderloin slices, chicken breast slices, mullet slices, medium-ripe pork loin slices, belly slices and squid slices in water. Ingredients are pea tip, leek, coriander, scallion, grass sprouts, ginger, magnolia slices, as well as Toufu slices. The staple food is rice noodles that are slightly scalded with water. It features goose fat cover, and soup boiling hot, but not steaming. It is rated as one of the "Top Ten Snacks in Kunming" by Yunnan Association of Catering and Gourmet Industry and Kunming Association of Catering and Gourmet Industry.

Baked Rice-flour Cake

Baked rice-flour cake is a local folk snack in Yunnan province. It is made of cooked rice pressed into lumps or round pancakes, baked over a charcoal fire, and then coated with sauce and stuffing. The recipe is the same as Ciba, but Ciba is made of glutinous rice and the rice-flour cake is made of rice. During the Republic of China, Zhai Yong'an, a Yuxi man, set up Yongshun Garden in Duanshi Street, Kunming, famous for selling this product exclusively. It is rated as one of the "Top Ten Snacks in Kunming" by Yunnan Association of Catering and Gourmet Industry and Kunming Association of Catering and Gourmet Industry.

Flower Cake

Flower cake is a kind of shortcake made of edible rose, which is unique to Yunnan province. It is a classic representative of Yunnan characteristics and is sold in local bakery stores in Yunnan. Flower cake is also one of the classic representatives of Yunnan style mooncake, one of the four major mooncake schools in China. The production of flower cake originated in the Qing Dynasty more than 300 years ago. The flower cake made of high-quality roses was listed as the imperial cakes because of its characteristic flavor, and was favored by Emperor Qianlong. The modern Dian style flower cake originated from the flower cake produced in Guansheng Garden of Kunming in 1945. At that time, a special field was set up in Xiba of Kunming to grow edible flowers for processing flower cake and rose candy.

Shilin Milk Cake

The famous Shilin milk cake is made of goat milk. It is one of the famous special foods in Yunnan. Shilin milk cake, produced in Shilin County, such as Guishan, Xijiekou, is a kind of high fat, high protein food. It is delicious, nutritious, convenient to eat and can be cooked into a variety of delicious dishes. Because it is easy to make and preseve, shilin milk cake is loved by people. There are many ways to cook it. It can be steamed, stewed, fried or eaten raw, or made into other beautiful and fresh dishes.

Modern Baba

Kunming modern baba originated from the "pretzels" in old Kunming. The legend has it that the shop had two modern girls knead dough with American butter, selling just-made hot pretzels, which were quite favored by customers for delicious taste. Customers did not know it was called pretzel, but the girls who sold it were dressed in a modern style, so they called it modern baba. Since then, it had spread to Kunming and became a brand of Kunming snacks. It was rated as one of the "Top Ten Snacks in Kunming" by Yunnan Association of Catering and Gourmet Industry and Kunming Association of Catering and Gourmet Industry.

Guandu Baba

Guandu Baba, originated in Guandu Ancient Town, is a local snack with Yunnan characteristics. It's a kind of baked pasta, stuffed by sesame, peanuts, walnuts and other finely ground nuts mixed with sugar. It is soft, sweet and delicious. In the busy market of Guandu, almost everyone holds a Baba, which is like a unique scenery in the ancient town.

Dudu Shaomai

Dudu Shaomai (Governor Shaomai) is a kind of marinated food originated in Yiliang, Kunming. Why was the Yiliang Shaomai titled Dudu Shaomai? Here's an interesting anecdote. According to the legend, during the Xuantong period of the Qing Dynasty, there was a restaurant named Zhushi Yingxingyuan in Yiliang City, specializing in cooking Shaomai and pickled vegetables, especially famous for Shaomai. Tang Jiyao, the governor of Yunnan Province, visited the shop to admire its reputation and tried Shaomai, which was later passed on as a good story. "Governor Shaomai" got its name from this. Dudu Shaomai tastes neither salty nor sour, although it has salt and vinegar as seasoning. The meat is rich but not greasy, and the filling is rich and juicy. It is also rated as one of the "Top Ten Snacks in Kunming" by Yunnan Association of Catering and Gourmet Industry and Kunming Association of Catering and Gourmet Industry.

Yiliang Roast Duck

Yiliang roast duck originated in the Ming Dynasty and has a history of more than 600 years. It is called "the leader of Yunnan cuisine", especially the "Dog Street Roast Duck" in Yiliang County. The roast duck is jujube red, crisp but not burnt, and the meat is tender and very delicious. In 2009, Yiliang duck was listed in the second batch of provincial intangible cultural heritage.

Think and Discuss:

有人说,没了烟火气,人生其实就是一段孤独的旅程。美食满足了我们的胃,温暖了我们的心,也美好了我们的生活。最受你青睐的美食是什么?你和它之间又有怎样的故事与情结?

第八节 深入人心昆明名片

提到能代表昆明的东西，众说纷纭，有的说石林，滇池，有的认为是云烟、白药。笔者认为最能代表昆明城市形象和文化内涵的非以下几个莫属。

（一）茶花

茶花是云南的省花，昆明的市花。在北国冰封雪飘，万花纷谢的隆冬季节，当你漫游云南，会随处可见如霞似火的山茶。满树火红的花，在绿色树叶的烘托下，更显得光彩照人。

昆明栽培山茶历史悠久，南诏、大理国时期，已成为重要的培植品种，元明之际，更加繁盛。文人墨客咏颂山茶的作品也非常多。目前，昆明山茶花的品种很多，花色也很多。邛竹寺、金殿、圆通山都有大片种植的茶花。每年花开时节，登山赏花已经成了昆明人喜欢的一项活动。

（二）红嘴鸥

1985年红嘴鸥首次来到昆明过冬，38年来昆明人与这群白色精灵相遇、相识、相守。红嘴鸥已成为这座西南名城一张靓丽的名片，而春城也成为红嘴鸥最温馨最眷恋的家园。在昆明越冬的主要有红嘴鸥和棕头鸥两种，进城的主要为红嘴鸥和少量的棕头鸥。红嘴鸥的种类、数量变化主要受其迁徙季节的天气和食物影响。

（三）翠湖

翠湖位于昆明市区五华山西麓，是城区的中心观光点。因其八面水翠，四季竹翠，春夏柳翠，故称"翠湖"。清康熙年间云贵总督范承勋、巡抚王继文于湖中建碧漪亭（俗称海心亭），水光潋滟，绿树成荫。湖中筑有东西堤和南北堤，把湖一分为四，湖中有海心亭，西侧有观鱼堂，东南有水月轩。翠湖堤畔旧有"十亩荷花鱼世界，半城杨柳抚楼台"之联，被誉为"城中碧玉"。

翠湖公园是市区最漂亮的公园之一，这里除了有独一无二的美景之外，还能让人感受到非常浓郁的文化氛围。退休的老人在这里尽情地吹拉弹唱，翩翩起舞，追求着自己的艺术梦想；艺术家、摄影爱好者在僻静的角落欣赏和构思着。

（四）大观楼长联

大观楼位于昆明市近华浦南面，是一座三层的木结构建筑。因其面临滇池，远望西山，尽览湖光山色而得名。乾隆年间，孙髯翁为其撰写长联，由名士陆树堂书写刊刻，大观楼因长联而成中国名楼。此长联也堪称"古今天下第一联"。

全联如下：

上联：五百里滇池，奔来眼底，披襟岸帻，喜茫茫，空阔无边！看：东骧神骏，西翥(zhù)灵仪，北走蜿蜒，南翔缟素，高人韵士，何妨选胜登临，趁蟹屿螺洲，梳裹就风鬟雾鬓，更苹天苇地，点缀些翠羽丹霞，莫辜负，四围香稻，万顷晴沙，九夏芙蓉，三春杨柳。

下联：数千年往事，注到心头，把酒凌虚，叹滚滚，英雄谁在！想：汉习楼船，唐标铁柱，宋挥玉斧，元跨革囊，伟烈丰功，费尽移山心力，尽珠帘画栋，卷不及暮雨朝云，便断碣残碑，都付与苍烟落照，只赢得，几杵疏钟，半江渔火，两行秋雁，一枕清霜。

上联意思是：五百里浩瀚的滇池，在我眼前奔涌，敞开衣襟，推开冠戴，这茫茫无边的碧波，多么令人欣喜啊！看吧：东方的金马山似神马奔驰，西边的碧鸡山像凤凰飞舞，北面的蛇山如灵蛇蜿蜒，南端的鹤山如白鹤翱翔。诗人们，何不选此良辰登上高楼，观赏那螃蟹似的小岛，螺蛳般的沙洲；薄雾中的绿树垂柳像少女梳理秀发一般摇曳，还有那漫天的水草，遍地的芦苇，以及点缀其间的翠绿小鸟和几抹灿烂红霞。尽情观赏吧！切莫枉费了滇池四周飘香的金色稻谷，明媚阳光下的万顷沙滩，夏日婀娜的莲荷，春天依依的杨柳。

下联意思是：数千年的往事，涌上我的心头，举起酒杯，仰对长空感叹，那些历史长河中诸多的英雄，而今还有谁在呢？试想：汉武帝为了开辟西南到印度的通道，在长安挖凿昆明湖操练水军；唐中宗派兵收复洱海地区，立铁柱以记功；宋太祖手挥玉斧，面对版图，将西南划在界外；元世祖率大军跨革囊木筏渡过金沙江，统一了云南。这些伟业丰功，真是费尽了移山的心力啊！但是朝代更替之快，犹如傍晚的雨，早晨的云一样的短暂，连幕帘都来不及卷起就很快消失了；就连那记功的残碑断碣，也都倾颓在夕阳暮霭之中。到头来，只留下几声稀疏的钟声，半江暗淡的渔火，两行孤寂的秋雁，一枕清冷的寒霜。

这副长联多至一百八十字，对仗工整，气势宏大，脍炙人口。上联写滇池及周围风光景物，歌颂昆明大好河山及农民的辛勤耕耘，只有劳动人民的业绩永久存在。下联联想云南历史，把封建王朝看作不长久的幻影，一朝跟着一朝兴起、衰亡，连幕都拉不及，最后只剩下些断碣残碑横卧在苍烟落日之中。上联描写滇池风光，下联写出云南历史，寓情于景，情景交融，浑然一体，堪称千古佳作。长联观物写情，内涵深刻，令人叫绝，被誉为"海内第一长联""古今第一长联""天下第一长联"等，一直流传不衰。

Section Eight Popular Name Cards of Kunming

When it comes to the representative of Kunming, there are different opinions. Some say Stone Forest and Dianchi Lake, while others think of

Yunyan and Baiyao. The author thinks the most representative Kunming city images and cultural connotations should be the following ones.

Camellia

Camellia is the provincial flower of Yunnan and the city flower of Kunming. When you travel in Yunnan, you can see camellias everywhere, like clouds and fire, blooming in the midwinter season when it is still frozen and flowers have disappeared in the north. The fiery red flowers, in the setting of green leaves, are even more radiant.

Kunming has a long history of camellia cultivation. During the period of Nanzhao and Dali, it had become an important variety of cultivation, and become more popular during the Yuan and Ming Dynasties. There are also many literary works singing camellias. At present, there are many kinds and colors of camellias in Kunming. There is a large scale planting in Qiongzhu Temple, Golden Palace and Yuantong Mountain. Climbing mountains to appreciate camellias has become a favorite activity in Kunming every year when they bloom.

Black-headed Gull

Since 1985, when black-headed gulls first arrived in Kunming for the winter, Kunming people have met, known and stayed together with these white spirits for 38 years. Black-headed gulls have become a beautiful name card of this famous southwest city, and Spring City has become the warmest and loving home of black-headed gulls. Black-headed gulls and brown-headed gulls are the main wintering species in Kunming, while black-headed gulls and a small number of brown-headed gulls enter the city. The number of black-headed gull species varies mainly due to the weather and food during its migration season.

Cuihu Lake

Cuihu Lake is located at the western foot of Wuhua Mountain, and is the key scenic spot of the city. It is called "Green Lake" because it has green water on all sides, green bamboos in all seasons and green willows in spring and summer. During the reign of Emperor Kangxi of the Qing Dynasty, Yungui Governor Fan Chengxun and officer Wang Jiwen built Biyi Pavilion in the lake, which is full of water and green trees. East-west as well as north-south dikes were built in the lake, which divide the lake into four parts. The beautiful view of fishes swimming around lotus and willows swaying lightly by pavilions can be seen here, hence winning the name "Jade in the City".

Cuihu Park is one of the most beautiful parks in the city, and visitors can not only appreciate the unique scenery but also feel the rich cultural atmosphere. Retired people could enjoy playing and dancing, pursuing their artistic dreams. Artists and lovers of photography could enjoy beautiful views and get inspiration.

Couplet on Grand View Tower

Grand View Tower, located in the south of Jinhuapu, is a three-story wooden building. Because it faces Dianchi Lake and is opposite to the West Mountain, it gives you both lake and mountain view, hence the name. During the reign of Emperor Qianlong, Sun Ranweng wrote the long couplet for it, and Lu Shutang, a famous scholar, wrote and engraved the long couplet, which made the Grand View Tower a famous building in China, and the long couplet is widely regarded as "the first longest couplet in the world".

The left roll means: the vast Dianchi Lake, 500 miles wide, is surging in front of my eyes. I open my gown and push away my crown, for I feel so much delightful at the boundless blue waves! Look: the Jinma Mountain in the east looks like a racing horse, the Rooster Mountain in the west is like a flying phoenix, the Snake Mountain in the north is like a winding snake, and the Crane Mountain in the south is just like a white flying crane. Poets, at this moment, why not climb a tall building and admire the crab-like island and the spiral-like sandbar; the weeping willows swaying in the mist just like a maiden combing her hair; the water plants extending to the edge of sky, the reeds everywhere, as well as green birds and a few brilliant red clouds dotted between them. Enjoy yourself! Do cherish the fragrant golden rice around Dianchi Lake, the vast expanse of sandy beach in the bright sun, the graceful lotus in summer, and the willows in spring.

The meaning of the right roll is: events thousands of years ago poured into my mind. I raised up my cup, and sighed to the sky that so many heroes in the long history have all gone. Just look back: in order to open up the passage from southwest to India, Emperor Wudi of the Han Dynasty drilled the water army in the Kunming Lake in Chang'an. Tang Zhongzong sent troops to recover Erhai area, and erected the iron column to record; Song Taizu, wielding a jade axe, faced the territory and drew southwest out of bounds; Yuan Shizu led the army to cross the Jinsha River by leather bags and wooden rafts, unified Yunnan. These great achievements were really made with efforts as great as moving mountains. But the alternation of dynasties is as swift as the evening rain, as brief as the morning clouds, and the curtain is soon gone before it can be rolled up. Even the monuments to the achievements are falling into the sunset, in the end, leaving only a few sparse bells, dim fishing fire in the river, two lines of lonely autumn geese, as well as cold frost at a night.

This long couplet has as many as one hundred and eighty words, neat antithetic imposing manner, hence winning universal praise. The left roll describes the scenery of Dianchi Lake and its surroundings, extols the great rivers and mountains of Kunming and the hard work of farmers as well as the achievements of the working people that exist forever. The right roll recalls the history of Yunnan, sees the feudal dynasty as a temporary phantom, one dynasty followed by another in rise and decline, even the curtain is not pulled, finally only some broken stones lying in the smoke of the sunset.

The couplet thus has won many honors including "the first longest couplet in China", "the first longest couplet in ancient and modern times", and "the first longest couplet in the world".

> **Think and Discuss:**
> 每个城市都有自己的城市特色和文化内涵，它们以无声的语言让人辨识出自己，是一张张城市名片。你喜欢的城市有哪些名片？你怎样看待它们和城市的关系？

第九节　英勇无畏昆明英雄

（一）闻一多

"你可知 Ma-cau 不是我真姓？我离开你太久了，母亲！但是他们掳去的是我的肉体，你依然保管我内心的灵魂。"还记得这首歌吗？它的创作者就是闻一多先生。

闻一多先生不是昆明人，却是昆明的英雄之一。1937 年 7 月，全国抗战爆发，时任清华大学中国文学系教授的他，随校迁往昆明，任北大、清华、南开三校合并后的西南联合大学教授。面对严酷的现实，他毅然抛弃文化救亡的幻想，积极投身到抗日救亡和争民主、反独裁的斗争中。"一二一"惨案爆发后，他亲自为烈士写挽词、送殡，并撰文揭露惨案真相。李公朴被暗杀后，他毫不畏惧，拍案而起，慷慨激昂地发表了《最后一次演讲》，并宣誓说：人民的力量是一定会胜利的，真理是永远存在的。闻一多先生在回家途中，遭遇埋伏，不幸遇难。

闻一多不仅是伟大的现代诗人、学者，还是伟大的爱国主义者，坚定的民主战士。

（二）聂耳

聂耳，原名聂守信，1912 年出生于云南省昆明市，中国音乐家。1935 年初创作了《义勇军进行曲》。他创作了数十首革命歌曲，他的一系列作品影响中国音乐几十年。他的音乐创作具有鲜明的时代感、严肃的思想性、高昂的民族精神和卓越的艺术创造性，为中国无产阶级革命音乐的发展指出了方向，树立了中国音乐创作的榜样。

聂耳是第一个写出中华人民共和国国歌的革命者；第一个为中华民族

和中国的劳苦大众写歌并在歌曲中创造了中国无产阶级形象的作曲家；第一个用电影音乐唤起民众用血肉筑起长城的电影音乐家和用群众歌曲的形式传达革命理想的作曲家；第一个用艺术歌曲的形式塑造中国劳动妇女的形象；第一个用儿童歌曲的形式呼唤新中国的作曲家。

Section Nine　　Brave and Fearless Heroes of Kunming

Wen Yiduo

"Did you know that Ma-Cau is not my real name? I have been away from you too long, mother! But they took my body, and you kept my soul." Remember that song? Its composer is Mr. Wen Yiduo.

Mr. Wen Yiduo was not born in Kunming, but he is one of the heroes of Kunming. In July 1937, when the War of Resistance Against Japanese Aggression broke out, as a professor of the Faculty of Chinese Literature at Tsinghua University, he moved to Kunming and became a professor of the Southwest Associated University. Facing the harsh reality, he resolutely abandoned the illusion of cultural salvation, and actively engaged in the struggle against Japan and the fight for democracy and anti-dictatorship. After the outbreak of the tragedy on February 1, 1945, he personally wrote for the martyrs, took part in funeral procession, and exposed the truth of the tragedy. When Li Gongpu was murdered, he was fearless, stood up to the case, passionately delivered the *Last Speech*, vowing that the power of the people is certain to win, the truth is always there. On his way home, Mr. Wen Yiduo was ambushed and killed.

Wen Yiduo is not only a great modern poet and scholar, but also a great patriot and a firm fighter for democracy.

Nie Er

Nie Er, born Nie Shouxin in 1912 in Kunming Yunnan, was a Chinese musician. In early 1935, he composed *March of the Volunteers*, which was chosen to be the national anthem of the People's Republic of China. He composed dozens of revolutionary songs and his series of works influenced Chinese music for decades. His music creation has a distinct sense of the times, serious thoughts, high national spirit and outstanding artistic creativity, which pointed out the direction for the development of Chinese proletarian revolutionary music, and set up an example of Chinese music.

Nie Er was the first revolutionary to compose the national anthem of the People's Republic of China; the first composer who wrote songs for the Chinese nation and the toiling masses of China and created the image of the Chinese proletariat in his songs; the first film musician who used film music to arouse the people to build a "great wall of flesh and blood", and the composer who used the form of popular songs to convey the revolutionary ideals. He is the first musician to create the image of Chinese working women in the form of art songs and the first to call for a new China in the form of children's songs.

Think and Discuss:

中华五千年的文明史中，涌现出了太多太多的英雄人物和英雄故事。请就你印象深刻的一个进行分享。

第二章　丽江篇①
Chapter Ⅱ　Lijiang

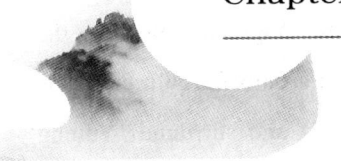

　　20年前，它藉藉无名，20年后，国内外的游客纷至沓来，这便是云南丽江。当地纳西话称丽江为"依古堆"，意为金沙江转弯的地方。金沙江似一条彩带，一头系着老君山，一头牵着小凉山，中间缠绕着玉龙雪山；长江第一湾又如同一个慈爱的母亲，怀里抱着丽江市，背上背着永胜县、宁蒗县和华坪县。

　　丽江位于青藏高原东南缘，横断山脉东部，滇西北中部，地貌复杂多样。山区、平坝、河谷等多种地貌类型并存，多样的地貌、明显的海拔高差使丽江兼有亚热带、温带、寒带三种气候。丽江全区大部分地方属低温带高原山区气候，冬无严寒，夏无酷暑。

　　丽江，这块2万多平方千米的红土地上居住着纳西、白、傣、傈僳、普米、苗族等22个少数民族，多姿多彩的民族文化资源和秀丽山川，像磁石般吸引着越来越多的中外游客慕名前往。东巴文化、纳西古乐、白沙壁画等已成为打造丽江旅游品牌与形象价值的独具魅力的当地旅游文化。

　　古代，丽江是汉唐时期南方丝绸之路和茶马古道上的重要集散地。如今，丽江是著名的旅游城市，是中国目前同时拥有世界文化遗产——丽江古城、世界自然遗产——三江并流和世界记忆遗产——东巴古籍的世界遗产圣地和世界遗产旅游胜地。

　　背起行囊，奔赴丽江，与它美丽相约。秀美玉龙雪山、梦幻蓝月谷、最美泸沽湖、时光古城、特色美食……等你来！

---

　　① 资料来源：影像云南：什么是丽江？星球研究所，云南学习平台，"学习强国"平台，2019年12月25日，摘自2021年8月18日。

Twenty years ago, it was unknown; 20 years later, more and more tourists at home and abroad come here for a visit, and this is the well-known city—Lijiang, Yunnan. Lijiang in Naxi language it is called "Yigudui", meaning the place at the turning point of Jinsha River, which like a colorful belt, connects Mount Laojun and Mount Liangshan on its two ends and surrounds Yulong Snow Mountain in its middle. And the First Bay of Yangtze River, like a kind-hearted mother, holds the city of Lijiang in her arms and the three counties of Yongsheng, Ninglang and Huaping on her back.

Lijiang is situated in the southeast of Qinghai-Tibet Plateau, in the east of the Hengduan Mountains (the mountain range running east-west), and in the middle of the northwest of Yunnan, making its landform various and complicated: mountainous areas, flat land and river valleys etc. co-exist in this area. Diverse landforms and obvious elevation difference make Lijiang enjoy three kinds of climate: subtropical zone, temperate zone and frigid zone. A large part of Lijiang belongs to the plateau-mountain climate in cryogenic zone, thus neither very cold in winter nor very hot in summer.

On this red land with more than 20,000 square meters live over 22 ethnic minority groups mainly including Naxi, Bai, Dai, Lisu, Pumi and Miao people. Rich and colorful ethnic cultures and pretty mountains and rivers have magnetized more and more tourists at home and abroad to visit here. Dongba culture, Naxi ancient music and Baisha mural have become the unique ethnic cultures of Lijiang for developing its tourism brands and enhance its image.

In ancient time, Lijiang was the major trade center along the Southern Silk Road and the ancient Tea-Horse Road. Today Lijiang has become a famous resort city, and it is especially the city of the world heritage and the tourist attraction of the world heritage with three world honors: The World

Cultural Heritage—Lijiang Ancient Town, The World Natural Heritage—The Cocurrent Flow of Three Rivers of Jinsha River, Lancang River and Nu River, and The World Memory Heritage—Dongba Ancient Books and Documents.

So carry your backpack and come to Lijiang for a romantic date. Graceful Yulong Snow Mountain, illusive Blue Moon Valley, beautiful Lugu Lake, time-survived Ancient Town and local delicacies…are awaiting you.

> **Think and Discuss:**
>
> 1. 我们该如何审视一座旅游城市的内涵？如何提升旅游的价值与意义？
>
> 2. 丽江不仅仅是一个旅游目的地，它还代表着一种生活态度与生活方式。你未来会选择生活节奏比较慢（如丽江）的城市，还是选择在诸如北京、上海、广州这些生活节奏快的城市奋斗？你认为一个城市的生活节奏会影响你的个人发展吗？

第一节 只此青绿，看一山一谷①

传说上天遗落了一颗蓝宝石，流落云南丽江玉龙雪山脚下，变成了这方土地上一汪多情的眼泪，这便是美得纯粹的蓝月谷，这是专属于丽江蓝月谷的一抹青色。在蓝月湖畔，随风行走，眼见之处都是这抹晕染开来的青。湖水清澈得让你不忍心打扰它的宁静。蓝天为画布，湖水便是天空之镜，蓝天白云全部映在这镜中。云在天上，也在水中，分不清哪里是水，哪里是天。水天一色的青，正是绝美的蓝月谷。

有水的地方怎能少了山的陪护？大自然巧妙地安排了一山一湖相遇，竟成了它最完美的杰作。这山便是丽江人心中的神山——玉龙雪山。身在丽江，只要稍稍仰起头，便可与玉龙雪山迎头相遇。它浓缩了全球中低纬度山岳冰川的精华，是世界上少有的城市雪山。宛如转动时令"万花筒"的玉龙雪山，四季绚丽，何止青绿。乘坐索道游览，便可真切感受玉龙雪山险、奇、峻的自然风貌。在这里，你可以闻到清新的空气，聆听到鸟唱虫鸣，看到雪山连绵、雪花飞舞。

玉龙雪山、蓝月谷是丽江人心中的家乡之美，更是游客向往的观光胜地。

Section One　The Beautiful Scenery of Yulong Snow Mountain and Blue Moon Valley

There's a legend that one blue gem was dropped from the Heaven and fell down at the foot of Yulong Snow Mountain in Lijiang, Yunnan, which turned

---

① 资料来源：云南丽江：只此青绿，看玉龙雪山. 丽江学习平台，"学习强国"平台，2022年03月04日，摘自2022年05月05日。

into a big drop of emotional tear, that is the present attractive Blue Moon Valley with the impressive color of blue. Once you visit here, you'll be obsessed with its tenderness and unforgettable beauty. Walking along the blue valley, you are surrounded not only with the gentle breeze but also with a piece of blue lying everywhere. While the blue sky as a large piece of canvas, the clear and tranquil water is like a mirror reflecting the blue sky and the cloud above. Then here comes a fancy that the cloud in the sky seems also in the water, hard to distinguish the water from the sky. And this is the Blue Moon Valley with its striking blue of both sky and its water.

With water always comes mountain, the beautiful encounter of one mountain and one valley is the nature's most skillful and perfect masterpiece. Behind the Blue Moon Valley is the holy Yulong Snow Mountain loved and respected by every Lijiang people. Wherever you are, looking up ahead, you can see it, which is the rarely existed snow mountain in city in the middle and lower latitude. The special location endows Yulong Snow Mountain with enough quintessence from mountains and glaciers in this area and creates a season kaleidoscope from which you can enjoy a colorful and wonderful snow mountain in four seasons except for the impressive blue. In a cable car, you can get a close touch with the mountain's heart-beating steepness and beauty. The fresh air, the pleasant singing of birds and insects, and the beautiful dancing snow flakes all belong here and belong to you.

For the local Lijiang people, here is the beauty of hometown; for the tourists in Lijiang, here is their longed-for tourist resort—Yulong Snow Mountain and Blue Moon Valley.

Think and Discuss:

大自然馈赠给每一个地方、每一个城市独特的美,你家乡的最美之处是什么?它的最美源于什么?

第二节 "中国桥"飞跃金沙江[①]

穿越60多年的风雨回望，从武汉长江大桥开始，一座座"中国桥"翻山越岭，穿江过海，创造了一个个"中国奇迹"。

金安金沙江大桥是丽江市境内连接永胜县与古城区的过江通道，位于金沙江水道之上，全长1386米，塔顶距离江面垂直高度479米，有170层楼高，桥面距离江面垂直高度335米，是世界最大跨径的山区峡谷悬索桥。在克服了云南金沙江地区高海拔、高地震烈度的复杂地质、地势与恶劣气候后，金安金沙江大桥于2020年12月31日通车试运营。该大桥是云南华丽（华坪至丽江）高速公路的控制性工程，该高速建成后，丽江至四川攀枝花行车时间从6小时缩短至2小时，丽江至成都车程缩短至9小时内，丽江到成都实现全线高速。

2022年4月13日，世界首座大跨度铁路专用悬索桥——丽香（丽江至香格里拉）铁路金沙江大桥主体工程全部完工。作为丽江至香格里拉铁路全线控制性工程，它是我国首座高山峡谷区铁路悬索桥。大桥全长882.5米，桥面至江面垂直距离约250米。大桥有望今年内开通。丽香铁路是滇藏铁路的重要组成部分，建成通车后，从昆明到香格里拉有望4小时抵达，丽江到香格里拉仅需1小时左右。

如今的中国大地上，一座座钢铁大桥正穿越崇山峻岭，横跨江河湖海，让人们享受着交通便利带来的美好生活。高山峡谷间一座座各式各样的桥梁，连通的不仅仅是城市，更连通了群众与人心。

[①] 资料来源：丽香铁路金沙江大桥主体工程完工.胡晓荣，谢明，谢珍.云南学习平台，"学习强国"平台，2022年4月16日，摘自2022年05月05日。

Section Two　The Chinese Bridges Spanning over Jinsha River

Looking back to the past 60 years of China's bridge building history, it was full of winds and rains. But starting with the rising Wuhan Yangtze River Bridge, one and another Chinese bridge has treked over mountains and hills and gone across rivers and seas, achieving one and another Chinese wonder.

Over the Jinsha River in Lijiang spans a bridge, the Jin'an Jinsha River Bridge, which is the river path in Lijiang connecting Yonsheng county with Ancient Town district. The bridge has a length of 1,386 meters with the vertical height of 479 meters from the river to its tower top, equivalent to the height of a 170-storey building, and the vertical height of 335 meters from the river to its floor. The bridge, as the suspended bridge with the world biggest span in the mountainous area, overcoming the complicated geological conditions of high altitude and being prone to earthquakes as well as adverse climate, finally held its opening ceremony on December 31, 2020 and commissioned its traffic operation. As the control project of Huaping-to-Lijiang highway, its completion shortened the previous 6 hours' journey from Lijiang, Yunnan to Panzhihua, Sichuan to the present 2 hours, and the driving time from Lijiang to Chengdu was shortened to less than 9 hours, realizing the full cover of highway from Lijiang to Chengdu.

The principal project of another bridge, the world first big-span suspended bridge made for railway, the Jinsha River Bridge of Lijiang-to-Shangri-la Railway was finished on April 13, 2022. This bridge is the control project of Lijiang-to-Shangri-la railway and the first suspended railway bridge in the mountainous area in China with the length of 882.5 meters and the vertical height of about 250 meters from the river to the bridge floor. As the major component of Yunnan-to-Tibet railway, it's estimated to be completed at the end of 2022, then the driving time between Kunming and Shangri-la will be 4 hours and about 1 hour only from Lijiang to Shangri-la.

Today, on the land of China, more and more bridges made of steel and iron are going through mountains and hills, and are going across rivers, lakes and seas, which have facilitated people's lives and connected one city with another as well as people's hearts.

Think and Discuss:

要致富，先修路，交通承载着人们对美好生活的向往。中国桥在世界舞台的步伐越迈越大，这背后是一代代桥梁专家的心血付出。请查阅了解被誉为"中国桥魂"的茅以升老先生，讲述他与中国桥的故事和他勇于创新、攻坚克难的精神。

第三节　智慧古城　民居智慧

丽江大研古城始建于宋末元初，距今已有 800 余年。丽江古城既无规则的道路，又无森严的城墙，设计精妙、风景宜人，是中国罕见的保存较为完好的少数民族古城。以相当于贸易广场的四方街为中心，街巷向四周散射。从城北黑龙潭流出的泉水被分为三股支流，三股支流再分成更小的分支，形成一个网状水系，穿街过巷。365 座石桥木桥跨水连街，河、街相伴，既保证了各处居民用水，也美化了城镇环境。

丽江古城选建在象山南麓、狮子山东麓、金山坝子西北角。此选址营造出"山、水、城一体"的丽江古城，整体格局体现出四大优越性：一是避风、向阳、暖和；二是依山傍水建城；三是居于丽江盆地中央，交通发达，商贸兴隆；四是周边群山环抱，又有东西北三面金沙江天险作为护城河，极具军事防御优势和安居乐业的环境。

丽江古城地处滇川藏交汇的核心地区，历史上是滇西北政治经济文化的中心，是汉唐时代通往印度、尼泊尔等地的南方丝绸之路和茶马古道上的重镇。如今，集世界文化遗产、国家历史文化名城、国家 5A 级景区、全国文明风景旅游区四张"金名片"于一身的丽江古城，享誉中外。

古城民居依街而建，依山势、水势和居家用途不同呈现出丰富多彩的格局，所有房屋都是土木结构，石脚高砌，木架支撑，土坯砌墙，木板隔整，灰瓦白墙，主屋一般坐北朝南。这样的建筑设计使房屋具有向阳采光、冬暖夏凉、防潮防震的优点。古城街道通小巷，条条小巷牵系着万户门洞，一入门洞，四合五天井，三房一照壁的建筑格局即呈现眼前。这些建筑有北京四合院的韵味，又有江南水乡的引水入户、活水绕屋的风情，整洁而又清幽宁静。房屋门窗配以精心雕刻的各式各样的图案。每一院房子的布

局、雕刻都是古城居民集体智慧创造的艺术品。

　　古城街道一律用五花石铺路，数百年后路面依然光滑透亮，使古城之路成为一道亮丽的风景。古城水多桥也多，源于象山西麓的玉泉水如肌体之血脉贯通全城，无处不在，使古城充满灵气、秀气、生气。

　　丽江古城的房屋、街道、水利建筑，无论从格式、格调，到选材、用材，都体现出尊重自然、亲和自然、利用自然的"天人合一"的思想观念。国内外建筑专家和大师都对古城的规划设计艺术给予了高度评价，赞叹不已。

Section Three The Wisdom in Lijiang Ancient Town and Its Folk Buildings

　　Lijiang Ancient Town was built during the late Song Dynasty and early Yuan Dynasty with a long history of over 800 years. It has no strictly-designed streets nor strictly-guarded walls and it is the rare well-reserved ethnic ancient town in China with intelligent and delicate layout as well as pleasant scenery. Centered around the Square Street that is considered as "Trade Square" in Lijiang Ancient Town, all streets stretch into all directions. The spring water from Heilongtan in the north of the town runs in three branches and then forms a network of water by running in more branches through the streets and lanes in the town. There are 365 stone bridges and wood bridges ingeniously connecting rivers and streets, which offers dwellers in every corner of the town enough water and also beautifies the town.

　　Lijiang Ancient Town has a sublime location at the southern foot of the Elephant Mountain, the eastern foot of the Lion Mountain and at the northwestern corner of Jinshan Basin. The unique location constructs a city surrounded by mountains and waters, which has four superiorities: first, less wind but more sunshine, thus warm; second, construction surrounded by mountains and waters; third, the location in the center of Lijiang Basin brings convenient transportation and flourishing business; fourth, even though the town has no strictly-guarded walls, it is still endowed with a safe and comfortable environment by being surrounded by mountains and guarded by Jinsha River in three directions of east, west and north like a natural "city moat".

Located in the heart of the converging point of Yunnan, Sichuan and Tibet, Lijiang Ancient Town, in history, is the political, economical and cultural hub in the northwest of Yunnan, and in the Han and Tang dynasties, is the pivotal town along the Southern Silk Road and the ancient Tea-Horse Road to India, Nepal and other nations. Today, as an ancient town owning four prestigious titles: the World Cultural Heritage, the National Historical and Cultural Town, The National 5A Level Scenic Spot, and the National Civilized Sightseeing Area, it has become world-famous.

The folk buildings in the Ancient Town are built along the streets and display different rich layouts by making full use of the natural condition of mountains and waters and by considering the practical function. All houses are of wood structure, with mud-brick-made white walls and gray tiles on the roof with wood pillars as the house prop and planks as the room separation, and the wall up from the ground is firmly strengthened with stone foundation. Such structure and layout like the principal room usually facing south give houses more sunshine and light, making the houses neither too cold in winter nor too hot in summer, and also dampness-proof and quake-proof. The streets and lanes in the town are ingeniously connected, and each lane can guide you to a house whose layout is either four rooms separately built with 5 courtyards or two-storey rooms in three directions (usually north, west and east) and a screen wall facing the south. The buildings of such architecture layout are tidy and peaceful, bearing both the style of Siheyuan, a type of Chinese residence commonly seen in Beijing, capital of China, and the water villages' peculiarity of bringing water into yard in the lower reach regions, south of Yangtze River. Besides the layout, various delicately-carved patterns on doors and windows are what Naxi folk buildings are characterized by, and every building can be an art work of the town dwellers' collective wisdom.

The smooth and bright streets in Ancient Town even after several hundreds of years are also something scenic for the material of five-colored stones. In Ancient Town, water and bridges are everywhere, and the Yuquan spring water from the western foot of the Elephant Mountain, like the blood vessel of the town, runs through every corner and makes the town full of vitality.

Ranging from the structure to the style and the material, the buildings, streets and water conservancy constructions in Ancient Town are the best manifestation of Naxi people's reverence for nature, friendliness to nature and the ideal that man is an integral part of nature. No wonder, its design has won great praise and good comment from the architecture professionals and masters both at home and abroad.

Think and Discuss:

1. 随着中国城市化进程与现代化步伐加快,"绿色环保"已经成为中国建筑生态文明思想之核心。坚定不移走生态优先、绿色发展之路,用绿色建造魅力、美丽中国建筑,让住在里面的人们感受自然的"绿色风景"已经成为中国建筑工程师们的建筑理念与夙愿。

2. 建筑是一个城市重要的形象名片,你如何评价你家乡的建筑?建筑应该如何与当地的文化、生态文明建设和谐统一发展?

第四节 舌尖记忆 品老味道

老味道总是充满魅力，因为它包含着人们过去的情感，也以味觉的方式记录着过去。丽江粑粑、鸡豆凉粉、三川火腿……这些富有丽江特色的美食等着您来品尝、品味。

（一）丽江粑粑

作为当地独具特色的美食之一，丽江粑粑历史悠久，外黄内酥，香味扑鼻，吃起来酥脆可口。口味一般分为甜、咸两种，前者配以白糖、芝麻、核桃仁等佐料煎烤而成，后者主要配以火腿末煎烤而成。根据个人口味不同，还可以配上酥油茶、豆浆、牛奶、咖啡等，是老幼皆宜的风味小吃。

（二）鸡豆凉粉

鸡豆凉粉是一种用豆类磨面滤浆做成的小吃，在丽江新老城区的大街小巷都能吃到，可谓经久不衰。俗话说，暑吃凉，寒吃热。拌以酸醋、葱花、蒜末、辣椒等调料，凉吃鸡豆凉粉，不仅爽口，还能够消暑开胃。鸡豆凉粉还可以热吃，将凉粉在平底锅内用香油双面炸黄，再拌上调料，又是一种美味。

（三）三川火腿

三川火腿产自丽江永胜县三川坝，因此得名。三川火腿是滇西火腿中的名品。从杀腊月猪，到割腿腌制都有一整套完整工艺。火腿风干后捂在栗炭灶灰中保存，时间越长，香味越足。腌制一两年后，便可成就色泽鲜红，肥而不腻，口感极佳的老火腿，可以炖、炒、蒸、煲汤，无论哪一种烹饪手法，都是上好佳品。

（四）永胜水酥饼

永胜水酥饼蕴藏着丽江市永胜县悠久的历史和文化，其传统手工技艺入选了云南省非物质文化遗产代表性项目名录。它色泽诱人，香酥松软，味道鲜美，是居家面点佳品，更是馈赠亲朋好友的理想选择。如今，在原有水酥饼的基础上，发展出来了五仁红豆、水果、蜂蜜、火腿等系列的水酥饼，种类丰富，选择更广，深受大家喜爱。

Section Four The Memory on the Tip of Tongue—The Unforgettable Taste

The unforgettable taste, for its accumulated rich emotions and feelings, is full of unique charm and is a special way of recording the past. The delicacies belonging only to Lijiang are awaiting you to taste and experience: Lijiang pan cake, Jidou bean jelly, Sanchuan ham and so on.

Lijiang Pan Cake

Lijiang pan cake, one of the distinctive local foods, has a long history, attractive golden yellow outside and fragrant and crisp taste. By different ingredients, there are two kinds: the sweet cakes and the sour ones. The sweet ones are mainly made of sugar, sesame and walnuts, and the sour ones are mainly made of ham. While eating, different people can have their own way by combining different ingredients like the local butter tea, soybean milk and coffee, etc. So Lijiang pan cake is really a delicious food for every age group.

Jidou Bean Jelly

Jidou bean jelly is a kind of local time-honored food by grinding Jidou beans (a kind of local wild beans rich in melanin), which can be seen everywhere in the city of Lijiang. There is a saying that the cool food is for hot weather and the hot for cold weather. This is true with Lijiang Jidou bean jelly. It can be eaten cold served with vinegar, green onion or garlic paste and chilli source, etc., which is good in taste, appetitive and can prevent heatstroke. Jidou bean jelly can also be eaten hot by baking it until it turns golden yellow outside and combing with the ingredients mentioned above, which is a different taste.

Sanchuan Ham

Sanchuan ham, the representative ham in the west of Yunnan, is named after its birthplace, the Sanchuan plain in Yonsheng county, Lijiang. From killing the New Year pigs to salting the pork legs, its making is a crafty and skillful process. After being dried in wind, they will be preserved in the stove ash until they smell specially fragrant. One or two years will give the hams fresh red outside and good taste. And the cooking can be various including stewing, stir-frying, steaming, and soup-making, either of which will make the best-tasting Sanchuan ham.

Yonsheng Shuisu Cake

Yonsheng Shuisu cake, storing the history and culture of Yonsheng, Lijiang, is a popular local snack. Its traditional craft has been listed in Yunnan Intangible Cultural Heritage items. For its attractive outside and crisp taste, it has become the best choice for family flour cooking and the gift to relatives and friends. Today, various Shuisu cakes have been developed like the ones made with five-nuts and red beans, the fruit cakes, the honey cakes and the ham cakes, which offer rich choices and thus becomes more and more popular with both the locals and tourists.

Think and Discuss:

1. 每一个地方的特色饮食不仅仅是一种味道，更是一代人的一种特殊记忆。你记忆中的家乡美食是什么？它带给你怎样的一种乡愁与情怀？

2. 有人说：人世间，唯有爱与美食不可辜负。你如何理解这句话？如何体悟爱与美食之间的关系？

第五节　古乐之韵　音乐活化石

　　纳西古乐是中华民族最古老、最珍贵的音乐文化遗产之一，是中国和世界的音乐精品，被称为音乐活化石。纳西古乐主要由唐宋时期的道教宫廷音乐、儒家雅集型细乐和词曲牌音乐组成。国内有关学者通过研究证实纳西古乐确实是唐宋遗音，此乃纳西古乐的价值。纳西古乐使用的乐器除管、弦、敲击乐器外，还有曲项琵琶、火不思、铜铃、波伯等特色乐器，其中不少乐器为数百年的文物。或许现代人无法欣赏古老的纳西古乐，但古老、朴素、纯真、雅致的音乐风格使纳西古乐保留下来了最难保存、最有价值的中华古代音乐文化遗产，传承和保留了这种超越时空的无形文化遗产。

　　提到丽江纳西古乐，不得不提及音乐怪才宣科。毫不夸张地说，没有宣科就没有纳西古乐今日的名声。1981年，年届花甲，对纳西族传统音乐有相当研究的宣科先生独具慧眼，带头组建了丽江中国大研纳西古乐会，并担任会长，使藏在滇西北高原的音乐活化石纳西古乐大放异彩，蜚声中外。被称为音乐怪才的他没有进过任何音乐学府，20岁就当过昆明文工团的指挥，历经人生坎坷后，他依然生气勃勃。

　　如今已至耄耋之年的他，依然挚爱音乐，活得年轻。宣科最大的贡献是通过不屈不挠、锲而不舍的努力，救活旷世绝响，把纳西古乐传承和宣传开来并走向世界。

Section Five　The Living Music Fossil—Naxi Ancient Music

　　Naxi ancient music, one of the oldest and most precious national music heritages of China, is considered as a living fossil and is the music classic in

China and the world. It is mainly made up of Taoist palace music, Confucian low-sound music played by pipes and strings, and epigraph and tune music during the Tang and Song dynasties. There's enough evidence that Naxi ancient music is actually the remained part of Tang and Song music, which is of great value. Its instruments include orchestral instruments and percussion instruments, and some distinctive instruments like Quxiang lute, Huobusi (a kind of strumming instrument used by ancient tribal groups), copper bell, and Bobo (an instrument similar to Oboe made of bamboo), many of which are cultural relics with a history of over a hundred years. For modern people, Naxi ancient music may be hard to catch, while its plain, innocent and graceful style helps to keep until today the most invaluable intangible music cultural heritage of ancient China that is hard to preserve but survives time and space eventually.

Speaking of Naxi ancient music, a person has to be mentioned. He is Mr. Xuan Ke, who became popular as Naxi ancient music developed and made a great contribution to its world reputation. In 1981, Mr. Xuan Ke in his sixties, had accumulated much research about Naxi traditional music, which motivated him to organize the Dayan Naxi Ancient Music Association, Lijiang, China, with himself as the first chairman. Afterwards, a living music fossil hidden in the plateau of northwestern Yunnan became well-known both at home and abroad. But actually the so-called music talent had never studied in a single music college or institute. At age of 20, he worked as the conductor in Kunming Art Troupe.

Now, Xuan Ke, in his nineties, is still energetic and keen on music. With his unremitting efforts, the endangered Naxi Ancient Music revived, and by his promotion and inheritance the music has taken up a part on the world stage, which is the greatest contribution made by him.

Think and Discuss:

1. 音乐已经成为每个人生活中必不可少的一部分，不论年龄、不分国界，是跨越语言、穿越心灵的一门世界性的语言。音乐也是文化的一种呈现方式。你如何理解音乐与生活以及文化之间的关系？

2. 20世纪90年代，"韩流"进入中国。广义的"韩流"包括韩国服饰、饮食等。狭义的"韩流"则通常指韩国电视剧、电影、音乐等娱乐事物的地区性影响。"韩流"从进入中国至今，对中国年轻人产生了极大的影响。你如何评价这种现象？

第六节　妙手匠心　剪出精彩

剪纸艺术是灿烂的纳西文化艺术中一枝绚丽的花朵。纳西人民的剪纸艺术同其历史风俗有着十分密切的联系，它真实反映了纳西人民丰富的思想感情和对美好生活的向往。纳西人民的剪纸艺术，吸收了汉、白、藏的优秀艺术成果，多出现于节假日或婚丧寿辰。民间较为广泛的是剪寿字。寿字，是长久、吉祥长寿之意。寿字在纳西人生活中的应用范围极为广泛，因此村村寨寨都有会剪寿字的民间艺人，也涌现出了一批优秀的剪纸艺人。纳西剪纸艺人凭自己丰富的想象和艺术素养，大胆地创造和捕捉，用简练明快的手法，以流畅的线条创造出一幅幅巧夺天工的剪纸艺术作品，为这一民间艺术之花的绚丽发展灌注了莫大心血。

Section Six　The Art of Paper-Cutting

Paper-cutting is an important component of Naxi people's cultural art. Closely related to their historical customs, Naxi people's paper-cutting is a mirror of their effusive thoughts and emotions as well as a prospect for a rosy life. Naxi people's paper-cutting is the result of taking in the excellent art of Han people, Bai people and Tibetans. It is commonly seen on special days like festivals, holidays, weddings, funerals and birthday celebrations, etc. And what's more widely seen is the cutting character "Shou" (a connotation of longevity and auspiciousness), which is widely used in daily life and there are many folk artists good at cutting "Shou", thus a group of excellent paper-cutting artists appearing. These artists, with their rich imagination, artistic quality, bold innovation and proficient handicraft, have created many wonderful paper-cutting art works in smooth lines, and they indeed have devoted as much as possible to the brilliant development of the folk art of paper-cutting.

> **Think and Discuss:**
>
> 剪纸艺术在中国由来已久,不同的地方拥有自己独特的剪纸技艺,也用不同的方式守护并传承着自己的剪纸文化。你认为剪纸等传统艺术应该如何从娃娃抓起?从而"剪"出文化,"剪"出守护,"剪"出传承?

第七节 丽江金沙陶 指尖记忆

云南省风景如画,风物独到,其制陶历史由来已久,拥有多项制陶技艺的国家非物质文化遗产:红河畔的建水紫陶、香格里拉的尼西黑陶、西双版纳的傣族慢轮陶、玉溪的青花瓷、丽江古城的金沙陶……以丽江当地纳西东巴文化为创作背景的金沙陶,逐渐形成了独特的风格。在丽江古城街头,挂满了大大小小具有当地文化特色的陶器制品。岁月经年,伴随着旅游业的兴起,丽江金沙陶作为饶有地域文化特色的工艺品,逐渐走红。在小小的民间制陶工艺坊中,制陶工具极其简单,很小的擀面棍、小竹棍,用手捏制而成,风干后再拿到后间进行烧制,每一个手工工艺品都独一无二,哪怕是出自同一双手,也无法复制出相同的作品。丽江金沙陶,有了纳西东巴文化元素的包装,让原来平淡无奇的土陶,成为具有文化底蕴的"指尖的记忆"。

Section Seven　Lijiang Jinsha Pottery-Making: Handmade Memory

Except for charming scenery and unique climate and landscape, Yunnan has a long history of pottery-making and many pottery-making arts have been listed as the national intangible heritage, including the Purple Clay Pottery of Jianshui in Honghe Yi Autonomous Prefecture, the Black Pottery of Nixi in Shangri-la, the Manlun Pottery of Dai in Xishuangbanna, the Blue-and-White Porcelain in Yuxi, and the Jinsha Pottery in Lijiang Ancient Town...

Characterized by Lijiang Naxi Dongba culture, Jinsha pottery has its unique style, and such pottery products of different sizes can be seen everywhere in Ancient Town. With the flourishing tourism in Lijiang, Jinsha pottery has become popular as the handiwork with local feature. Pottery-making tools are as simple as a rolling flour pin or a bamboo stick. In a small workshop, a pottery is finished by hands, and then is burned after being dried. There's no one pottery handiwork the same as another despite being made by one pottery-maker. Jinsha pottery has become the "hand made cultural memory" from local common pottery by integrating Naxi Dongba culture elements.

Think and Discuss:

你家乡的非遗传统技艺有哪些？在如今"互联网+"的时代，当非遗遇上互联网，传统技艺如何焕发新的生命力？从大学生的角度谈谈你的想法。

第八节 以赉化友 古朴纯美

"化赉"一词为当地纳西语,"化"为一群体,"赉"为每人拿出东西合在一起,意为一群体拿出东西相互帮助。过去化赉有米化赉、肉化赉、钱化赉、酒化赉、布化赉等。"化赉"是在自觉自愿的基础上,熟人、朋友等相识相知之人拿出一定同等数额的钱物凑集在一起,帮助群体中的赉友。哪一个赉友家庭发生困难,哪一个赉友先拿"赉",以便克服急用之难。同时,赉友之间利用化赉时相聚的机会,可以相互沟通感情,凝聚友谊。化赉这一以相互帮助为主要目的的传统美德文化承传至今。如今,这种风俗有了新的变化。随着人们生活水平的提高,赉友之间物质上的帮助已不再是主要目的,而是以交流感情为主要内容,因此,赉钱也只是一种联系的媒介而已。赉友的形式以同学、同事、老乡为主,有小学同学赉、中学同学赉,也有儿时伙伴赉。每逢周末休息之机(已退休的老年人无论节假日,只要有兴趣,都会组织聚会),以化赉为媒介约起来,轮流拿赉,谁家拿赉,就到谁家相聚,或者由拿赉者选定在外用餐地点,购买糖果糕点。化赉会上,大家谈心、玩麻将等。赉后,大家会将一定数额的赉钱统一交给拿赉者。如今,化赉不再局限于当地人民。化赉不仅是传统集体文化观念的再现与传承发展,作为丽江特有的一种古朴纯美的民间风情,也是纳西人民热爱生活、助人为乐、善待人生的精神反映。

Section Eight   The Local Unique Get-Together—Huacong

Huacong is the calling by local Naxi people, "Hua" means a group of people, "cong" means every member in this group gives away something, and together means offering mutual help within a group by offering something per person. In the past, the content of "cong" could be rice, meat, money, wine, cloth, etc. "Huacong" is a voluntary activity and happens among familiar friends or acquaintances who offer a certain sum of money to help the members. The member in need of help usually get the money first, namely cong, to overcome the difficulty he is confronted with. Meanwhile, members can exchange with each other to make themselves closer by this get-together. Today, with the improvement of people's living standard, new changes have been added to the inherited traditional virtue and culture whose original purpose is offering material help to members, which has been replaced by emotion exchange between members. In this regard, money offered by each member is just a media to associate. Members of Huacong can be various, mainly including classmates like those in a same primary school or in a same middle school, co-workers and townpeople as well as those who grow together since young. Usually on weekends, people will get together by Huacong and take turns to get money (cong), while for the retired people, their get-together is not limited by time, whenever interested, a Huacong can be organized. Anyone who takes turn to get money (cong) is supposed to choose where to get together, either in his home or out, and prepare snacks like fruits, candies, cakes and pastries. While getting together, people have a casual chat or play Majiong, after dinner, members will give the money negotiated before to the one who organized Huacong. Nowadays, the custom is not only for the locals.

As a unique local folk custom in Lijiang, Huacong is not only a re-representation, inheritance and development of Naxi people's traditional idea of collective culture, but also a full reflection of their great love for life, their good qualities of helping others and a positive life attitude.

Think and Discuss:

聚会,如亲友聚会、同学聚会、老乡聚会在现代人的生活中日益普遍,吃、喝、玩、乐更是成了年轻人聚会的主要形式与内容。对此,你如何看?在物质丰盈的现代社会,我们应该如何提升聚会的品质与意义?

第三章　大理篇
Chapter Ⅲ　Dali

　　大理白族自治州位于云南省中部偏西，州府驻地大理市下关，距昆明市 331 千米。自治州总面积 29 459 平方千米，其中山区面积占 93.4%，坝区面积占 6.6%。全州辖大理市、漾濞彝族自治县、祥云县、宾川县、弥渡县、南涧彝族自治县、巍山彝族回族自治县、永平县、云龙县、洱源县、剑川县、鹤庆县，共 1 市 11 县，110 个乡镇。

　　大理州地处云贵高原与横断山脉的交汇地带，地势西北高东南低，境内山川广布，江河纵横，风光无限。以中部苍山为界，东西两侧地貌、景观大不相同。西部澜沧江、怒江流域，山高谷深，景色壮丽；东部金沙江流域地势平阔，沃野星罗棋布。高山盆地间错落分布着洱海、天池、茈碧湖、西湖、东湖、剑湖、海西海、青海湖 8 个湖泊。其中洱海是云南省第二大内陆淡水湖泊，风光明媚，素有"高原明珠"之称，与苍山一起被列为国家级风景名胜区。

　　大理州地处低纬高原，在低纬度、高海拔地理条件的共同影响下，形成年温差小、四季不明显的气候特点。"四时之气，常如初春，寒止于凉，暑止于温。"全州由于地形地貌复杂，海拔高低悬殊，气候的垂直差异显著。气温随海拔高度增加而降低，雨量随海拔增高而增多。河谷热，坝区暖，山区凉，高山寒，立体气候明显。

　　大理是滇西要冲，一向被称为"亚洲文化十字路口的古都"。著名的南方丝绸之路与茶马古道在这里交汇，使大理成为连接东亚、南亚的重要交通枢纽，古代遗留下来的驿道、桥梁、马站随处可见。历史上大理与南亚、东南亚各国之间的文化交流和商贸往来都十分频繁。各方文化汇聚于此，经过千余年的交流碰撞，形成了高度发达的物质文化和高度开放包容的精神文化，因此大理又被誉为"多元文化与自然和谐共荣的典范"。

Dali Bai Autonomous Prefecture is located in the west-central part of Yunnan Province. Xiaguan, where its local government operates from, is 331 kilometers northwest of the provincial capital Kunming. The prefecture has a total area of 29,459 square kilometers, of which 93.4 percent is mountainous region and 6.6 percent is flatland. It consists of one county-level city (Dali), eight counties (Xiangyun, Binchuan, Midu, Yongping, Yunlong, Eryuan, Jianchuan, Heqing), three autonomous counties (Yangbi Yi Autonomous County, Nanjian Yi Autonomous County, Weishan Yi and Hui Autonomous County) and 110 towns.

Situated at the boundary between Yunnan-Guizhou Plateau and Hengduan Mountains, the prefecture drops in elevation as one travels from the northwest to the southeast. The landform is varied and complicated, with numerous mountains and rivers affording breathtaking views. With the Cangshan Mountain as a central dividing line, the east and west demonstrate totally different landscapes. The Lancang and Nujiang River basins in the west are magnificent with lofty mountains and deep valleys. The eastern Jinsha River basin is flat and expansive, dotted with fertile fields. Eight crystal alpine lakes, namely Erhai Lake, Tianchi, Cibi Lake, West Lake, East Lake, Jianhu, Haixi Lake and Qinghai Lake, are scattered among the mountains and rivers. Erhai Lake, the second largest inland freshwater lake in Yunnan Province, has been listed as a national scenic spot together with the Cangshan Mountain. It offers stunning scenery and is praised as the "Pearl of Plateau".

Owing to its geographical location with high altitudes and low latitudes, the four seasons here are indistinct and the temperature varies slightly during the year. There's no summer heat and winter chilliness. Vertical differences of climate are significant due to complex topography and huge elevation difference. The temperature decreases while the rainfall increases with elevation. It's hot in the valleys, warm on the flatlands, cool in the hills and cold on high mountains.

As a vital transportation hub in western Yunnan Province, Dali has been widely known as the "Ancient Capital at the Crossroad of Asian Culture". The famous Southern Silk Road and the ancient Tea-Horse Road converge here, making Dali an important junction connecting East Asia and South Asia. Post roads, bridges and horse stations from ancient times can be seen everywhere in the prefecture. Historically, Dali developed an extensive network of culture exchange and trade with South Asia and Southeast Asia. After thousands of years of interactions, a highly developed material culture as well as a highly open and inclusive spiritual culture have formed, shining brilliantly and attracting worldwide attention. This wins Dali a reputation as the "Model of Harmonious Coexistence of Diverse Cultures and Nature".

Think and Discuss:

区位优势在大理乃至整个云南的发展史上都发挥着重要作用。古代的南方丝绸之路和茶马古道共同带动了云南地区前进的脚步。2021年12月3日，中老铁路全线开通运营。这条作为"一带一路"标志的跨国性铁路北起云南昆明，途经玉溪、普洱、西双版纳，南至老挝首都万象。有人说中老铁路的贯通意义非凡，可以说是中老双赢铁路。对此你怎么看？你觉得这条铁路对中老两国、对东南亚地区意味着什么？

第一节　史海寻踪　古迹大理

大理拥有悠久的历史和灿烂的文化，州内文物古迹荟萃，是全国重点文物保护单位最多的少数民族自治州。大理古城是 1982 年国务院公布的第一批 24 个国家级历史文化名城之一。遍布大理各地的众多史前人类遗址、古城址、古塔、古寺庙、古碑刻等文化遗存，历经岁月洗礼而光彩不减，无声地诉说着过往的光辉岁月。

大理的历史最早可以追溯到遥远的新石器时代。20 世纪 30 年代以来，在以洱海为中心的两百多千米范围内，陆续发现了新石器时代和青铜器时代的文化遗址上百处，其中以宾川白羊村文化遗址、剑川海门口文化遗址、祥云大波那文化遗址等最为典型。这些文化遗存表明，早在几千年以前大理各族先民就已经在这里繁衍生息。

大理曾长期处在封闭自守、孤立发展的状态中，远离中央封建王朝的统治。直到西汉时期，汉武帝刘彻征服"西南夷"，才将大理正式纳入了中央王朝的版图。史载汉武帝为征服洱海周围善于水上作战的"昆明人"，在长安按照洱海的形状开凿"昆明池"操练水军。今昆明大观楼长联中记述的典故"汉习楼船"反映的就是这段历史。

唐宋时期是大理历史发展的重要阶段。"南诏国"和"大理国"两个地方政权相继在大理建都，前后延续 500 多年，几乎与唐宋王朝相始终。其间大理一直是云南的政治、经济、文化中心。位于今大理市太和村西的古太和城即建于此时期，曾为南诏都城，其遗址尚存南北两道城墙。太和城遗址立有"南诏德化碑"，是研究南诏历史文化的重要资料。"南诏德化碑"对唐王朝与南诏之间的"天宝战争"有较为详细的记述。此外，今下关天宝公园内的"大唐天宝战士冢"，苍山斜阳峰下供奉阵亡唐将李宓的"将军洞",以及"苍山会盟"旧址——位于苍山中和峰的"苍山神祠"也都是唐与南诏关系的见证。南诏后来迁都至羊苴咩城,其后大理国时期也一直将羊苴咩城作为国都。该城位于苍山中和峰下,范围约在今大理古城以西一带,尚能看到一小段城墙遗址。据史籍记载,羊苴咩城建筑规模宏大,环境优美,建筑工艺也达到了很高的水平。

南诏大理国时期大理地区的文化空前繁荣,留下的文物古迹非常丰富。大理崇圣寺三塔和剑川石钟山石窟就是该时期艺术瑰宝中的佼佼者。崇圣寺在大理国时期曾是皇家寺院,多位皇帝逊位之后在此清修。原崇圣寺建筑群已毁,仅留寺前鼎立的三座佛塔,历经千年风雨和数十次地震而不倒,充分显示了古代大理工匠高超的建筑艺术。三塔中的主塔名千寻塔,塔身呈纺锤形,建筑风格兼具地方和民族特色,是南诏大理国时期佛塔建筑的典范,此后的许多佛塔都是仿照千寻塔而建。剑川石钟山石窟有"西南敦煌"的美誉,是我国石窟艺术中的一颗明珠,也是反映南诏、大理国历史文化风貌的一幅优美画卷。

元世祖忽必烈率军攻灭大理国后建云南行省,迁省治到昆明。昆明大观楼长联中的另一典故"元跨革囊"说的就是元军利用传统的渡江工具羊皮口袋(即"革囊")巧渡金沙江的故事。今大理古城西门外的三月街广场留有"元世祖平云南碑",碑文追述了忽必烈平云南的经过,是研究元初云南政治、军事的重要史料。

明清以来,大理仍然是滇西重镇。明洪武年间在苍山中和峰下原羊苴咩城东侧修筑了大理城。历史上大理古城屡遭损毁,20世纪80年代曾重修城墙和城楼。如今登楼西望,田野阡陌中依稀可见千年前羊苴咩城的一段残垣。清咸丰、同治年间,回族领袖杜文秀起兵反抗清王朝的统治,建立政权,影响深远。起义军推举杜文秀为"总统兵马大元帅",今大理古城南门内有"杜文秀元帅府",位于古城东南的下兑村有"杜文秀墓"。

1956年大理白族自治州成立,大理的历史揭开了崭新的篇章,如今大理已成为滇西重要的交通枢纽和旅游中心城市。

Section One A Wealth of Historical Sites

Dali has a long history and a splendid culture. Among all the autonomous prefectures in China, it has the largest number of major historical and cultural sites protected at the national level. The Dali Old Town is one of the first 24 National Historical and Cultural Cities announced by the State Council in 1982. Numerous cultural relics, including prehistoric human sites, ancient cities, pagodas, temples and tablet inscriptions, are still shining all over the prefecture and demonstrating its glorious past.

Archaeological evidence confirms that the history of Dali goes as far back as the Neolithic Age. Since the 1930s, hundreds of Neolithic and Bronze Age sites have been found in an over-200-kilometer radius around the Erhai Lake. The most representative are the Baiyang Village site in Binchuan County, the Haimenkou site in Jianchuan County and the Dabona site in Xiangyun County. They indicate early humans had been living and thriving in this region for thousands of years.

Dali had long been in a state of closed and isolated, far from the rule of the central feudal government. It was not until the Western Han Dynasty that the region was brought under direct central control by its conqueror Liu Che, also known as Emperor Wu. According to historical records, in order to conquer the "Kunming people" who lived around Erhai Lake and were good at battling on the water, Emperor Wu dug a so-called "Kunming Lake" in Chang'an, which was actually an accurate imitation of Erhai Lake. This story is well reflected in an allusion (terraced warships teeming with Han soldiers) from the Lengthened Couplet of Daguan Pavilion in Kunming.

The development of Dali came to a critical stage during the time of Tang and Song empires. Nanzhao and Dali Kingdom established their capitals here in succession and existed almost in parallel with Tang-Song Dynasty over a period of more than 500 years, during which Dali remained the political, economic and cultural center of Yunnan. Taihe Old Town, once the capital of Nanzhao Kingdom, lies west of the Taihe Village which is a few miles south of Dali City. Stretches of its southern and northern walls are left for today's visitors. On the ruins of Taihe Old Town stands the Nanzhao Dehua Tablet, an important resource for the study of Nanzhao's history and culture. The tablet gives a detailed account of the Tianbao War between the Tang Empire and the Nanzhao Kingdom. Other witnesses to Tang-Nanzhao relationship include the Tomb of Tianbao Soldiers located in the Tianbao Park in Xiaguan, the Grotto of the General at the foot of Xieyang Peak of Cangshan Mountain and the Cangshan Temple at the foot of Zhonghe Peak. The Nanzhao Kingdom later moved its capital to Yangjumie, which was also made the capital by subsequent Dali Kingdom. It's recorded that the Yangjumie city was a spectacular architectural achievement. It was built at the foot of Zhonghe Peak, west of present-day Dali Old Town, and the remains of its city walls can still be seen today.

The Nanzhao and Dali Kingdom created unprecedentedly prosperous culture, with abundant relics and historic sites left behind. The Three Pagodas of Chongsheng Temple in Dali City and the Shizhongshan Grottoes in Jianchuan County are outstanding artistic treasures from this period. The Chongsheng Temple, where many emperors practiced Buddhism after their abdication, used to be an imperial temple in the time of Dali Kingdom. In front of the temple stand one big pagoda and two small pagodas in a symmetric triangle. The original temple was destroyed while the pagodas have survived dozens of earthquakes over a long history of more than 1,000 years, which fully demonstrates the superb workmanship of ancient people. The big pagoda, named Qianxun, is spindle-shaped and has a remarkable ethnic feature. It's a model of pagoda architecture during the Nanzhao and Dali Kingdom periods, and many other pagodas of later generations have followed its example. The Shizhongshan Grottoes, known as the "Dunhuang in Southwest China", are a pearl of Chinese grotto art, as well as a beautiful painting scroll depicting the history and culture of Nanzhao and Dali Kingdom.

The end of Dali Kingdom came with the invasion of Kublai Khan's army. Kublai set up Yunnan Province, with Kunming as its capital city. Another allusion from the Lengthened Couplet of Daguan Pavilion tells the story of Yuan soldiers crossing the Jinsha River on sheepskin rafts. A stone tablet was erected by Kublai Khan to commemorate his conquest of Yunnan, and it still stands on the Square of March Street outside the west gate of Dali Old Town as an important historical document for the study of Yunnan's politics and military affairs in the early Yuan Dynasty.

Dali continued to be an important city in western Yunnan during the Ming and Qing dynasties. The Dali Old Town was originally built at the foot of Zhonghe Peak, east of ancient Yangjumie city, in the fifteenth century during the Ming Dynasty. It was damaged for many times in history and rebuilt in the 1980s. Standing on the walls and looking to the west, one can see the ruins of Yangjumie from a millennium ago. During the reign of Emperor Xianfeng and Emperor Tongzhi in the Qing Dynasty, Du Wenxiu staged a Hui ethnic minority revolt against the feudal government and established a local regime. This rebellion had a far-reaching influence, and Du Wenxiu was elected Marshal of the Military Forces. The Marshal Mansion inside the south gate of Dali Old Town was home to Du, and an honorary tomb was constructed for him in Xiadui Village, southeast of Dali Old Town.

The Dali Bai Autonomous Prefecture was founded in 1956, since then a new chapter of the prefecture has been written. Today's Dali has become an important transportation hub and tourist center in western Yunnan Province.

> **Think and Discuss:**
> 大理历史悠久，名胜古迹众多，令人神往。你的家乡有什么重要的历史遗迹？你了解自己家乡的历史吗？保护文物古迹、历史风貌有什么积极意义？

第二节 异彩纷呈 文艺大理

大理拥有深厚的民间文化根基和多姿多彩的民间艺术形式。源远流长的民间文化艺术为后世光辉灿烂的文学艺术成就奠定了坚实的基础。

（一）打歌

"打歌"是白语的音译，意为"踏唱"，是一种边唱边跳的歌舞。其历史悠久，大约在秦汉之际就已经产生，目前多在盛大集会或节日的夜间进行。歌者分成两组，双方都由"歌头"领唱，围绕篝火边唱边跳，一问一答。打歌的调子没有严格的规律和音韵，句法也不固定；步法、动作都非常简单，没有太多复杂的变化。

（二）白族调

白族调是大理民歌的主体，是用白语吟唱的一种曲调，大部分当地人都会听会唱。大理民间各种集会和生产劳动时普遍流行对唱白族调。重大节日时，成千上万人聚在一起对唱，往往持续几天几夜，场面十分壮观。白族调题材广泛、格律严谨。从文学上来说，白族调的唱词已经形成了本民族独有的诗歌格律"三七一五"体，即每节歌词都有四句，前三句七言，后一句五言。它的起源可以追溯到南诏时期，元明之际逐渐成形。明代诗人杨黼创作的抒情长诗《词记山花·咏苍洱境》就是以这种格律写成，因而又被称为"山花体"。

（三）大本曲

大本曲是一种古老曲艺，在大理有广泛的群众基础，多为有人物和故事情节的长篇曲本，故名"大本曲"。曲本由唱词和说白两部分组成，以唱词为主，辅以少量说白。曲本与白族调一样主要是"三七一五"句式，即"山花体"式。内容多根据汉族的历史和民间故事改编而成，如《三国演义》《梁山伯与祝英台》。也有一些根据当地的神话传说、历史故事改编，如《白王的故事》《火烧松明楼》。传统的大本曲演出，通常由一人演唱，一人弹三弦伴奏。俗语说"三月三开曲门，九月九关曲门"。每年三月至九月是民间演唱大本曲的旺季。

（四）白剧

白剧原名吹吹腔，是全国仅存于大理的民族剧种。明清时在滇西地区已经相当流行，至今仍深受大理群众喜爱。白剧表演与我国其他的戏曲有共同之处，分"生旦净丑"不同行当，通常由唢呐、锣鼓、笛子等伴奏。白剧唱词的文学韵味很强，不少剧本出自文人手笔。唱词格律与其他地方戏曲不同，基本上都是"三七一五"的"山花体"。

（五）霸王鞭舞

霸王鞭舞是大理民间最流行的基本舞蹈，多在喜庆节日如传统的三月街和绕三灵活动中表演。男性表演者手持八角鼓，女性执霸王鞭，常常同台演出。霸王鞭是将铜钱嵌入竹棍两头而成，长约1米。竹棍上有纸花，舞蹈时能发出有节奏的响声。八角鼓边缘嵌有铜钱、铜铃，因此又称金钱鼓。表演时花样很多，节奏鲜明，步伐整齐。表演者边跳边吟唱白族调，气氛热烈欢快。南诏国时期因为开疆拓土，全民尚武，许多竞技性体育运动都含有练兵习武的元素。霸王鞭舞很可能就是南诏全民练武的遗风。

Section Two Brilliant Folk Arts

Dali is blessed with deep-rooted folk culture and brilliant folk arts, which lay a solid foundation for the very impressive literary and artistic achievements of later generations.

The Dage Dance

"Dage" means dancing and singing in the Bai language. The Dage Dance has its roots in the Qin and Han dynasties. Contemporary Dage performances usually take place on the nights of grand fairs and festivals. Performers are divided into two groups, each following a leading singer. They gather around the campfire, singing while dancing, asking and answering questions in turns. No rigorous rhyme schemes or fixed syntax are required in the Dage songs, and the footwork and movements are simple and largely unchanged.

The Bai Tune

Most Dali people are capable of singing the Bai tunes, a particular type of folk songs in the Bai language. The antiphonal singing of Bai tunes enjoys great popularity at various gatherings and people love singing them when laboring in the fields. On major festivals, thousands of people gather to sing day and night. The Bai Tune has a wide range of themes and strict metrical patterns. From literary point of view, its lyrics fit the unique Bai poetic style, which had its roots in the Nanzhao Kingdom and gradually took its shape during the Yuan and Ming dynasties. Each section of the lyrics has four sentences, there are seven words in each of the first three sentences and five words in the last. A particular example of this is a long poem, *The Poem of Shanhua Ode to Cangshan Mountain and Erhai Lake*, which was composed by Yang Fu, a poet in the Ming Dynasty. Yang's poem was so famous that this special form of poetry was called the "Shanhua Style" from then on.

The Daben Ballad

The Daben Ballad is a well-liked folk musical art combining singing and story-telling. "Daben" means "long script", and most Daben scripts are long stories. The scripts are composed of lyrics and narration. Like the Bai Tune, Daben Ballad follows the Shanhua Style. Most stories are adapted from historical stories and folk tales of Han people, such as "The Romance of Three Kingdoms" and "Liang Shanbo and Zhu Yingtai". Some are based on local history and folklore, like "The Story of the White King" and "The Burning of Songming Tower". Traditionally, the balladeer sings to the accompaniment of Sanxian, a three-stringed instrument. Most performances are available from the third to the ninth month of the lunar calendar, the peak season for Daben Ballad.

The Bai Opera

The Bai Opera, formerly Chui Chui Qiang, is an ethnic opera unique to Dali. It prevailed in western Yunnan during the Ming and Qing dynasties, and is still popular with contemporary Dali residents. Like other traditional Chinese operas, there are different roles in the Bai Opera: Sheng (male), Dan (female), Jing (male with a painted face) and Chou (clown). The performance is usually accompanied by instruments like suona, gong, drum and flute. The Bai Opera has a strong literariness and many plays are composed by men of letters and conform to the Shanhua Style.

The Whip Dance

The Whip Dance is the most classic dancing form in Dali, usually performed on traditional festival days, the March Street and Raosanling Festival. Male performers play octagonal in particular drums on the stage while females brandish the so-called Bawang whips. The one-meter-long whip is made of bamboo sticks decorated with coins and paper flowers at both ends, thus able to make rhythmic sounds in dancing. The octagonal drum is also called the Jinqian Drum by virtue of the coins and bells embedded on the edge. The Whip Dance performance is diverse and varied, featured by rhythmic steps and cheerful atmosphere. Performers dance as they sing the Bai tunes. Many competitive sports in Dali contain martial elements, which is also true for the Whip Dance. That's probably a legacy of the Nanzhao Kingdom which advocated martial arts training for the purpose of territory expansion.

Think and Discuss:

从牛年春晚到《元宵奇妙夜》，再到《清明奇妙游》《端午奇妙游》《七夕奇妙游》《中秋奇妙游》和《重阳奇妙游》，2021年河南卫视的多档晚会节目屡屡火爆出圈，获得广泛好评。你认为这些节目获得成功的关键是什么？在弘扬传统文化方面河南卫视的经验给了我们什么启示？你能策划一些活动来推广大理地区优秀的民间艺术吗？

第三节　文献名邦　人文大理

得益于悠久文化传统的熏陶，加之大理地区向来重视教育，因此州内历代英才辈出，成绩斐然，创造了光辉灿烂的文学艺术成就，也为大理赢得了"文献名邦"的美誉。

（一）《南诏图传》

《南诏图传》由图画和文字两部分组成，作于南诏中兴二年（公元899年），因此又称《南诏画卷》《南诏中兴国史画卷》。画卷内容主要是细奴逻发祥巍宝山的神话故事，笔法生动而富于变化。南诏时期各阶层人物的服饰神态均有表现，展现了丰富的想象力和深厚的艺术功底。图卷原藏于清朝宫廷，八国联军侵入北京时被盗走，今存日本京都"有邻馆"，国内只有复制照片。

（二）《张胜温画卷》

《宋时张胜温绘大理国梵像卷》，简称《张胜温画卷》，作于大理国时期，是世界佛教图像中的瑰宝。作者张胜温是大理国一位画师。画卷题材以佛教故事为主，同时反映大理国的外事活动。画卷绘有几百位不同人物。画中人物形象生动传神，笔画细腻工巧，用色讲究，光彩夺目，有"南天瑰宝"之誉。有学者认为其画风与敦煌壁画属同一系统，说明当时大理国受中原文化影响很深。《张胜温画卷》后来流入中原，清乾隆时收入皇宫珍藏，1944年曾在重庆展出，后来被带到台湾，现藏于台北故宫博物院。

（三）"山花体"诗人杨黼

杨黼是明代诗人、学者、书画家，一生不求功名，终身隐逸。他的代表作《词记山花·咏苍洱境》是一首白文长诗，赞美苍洱风光，抒发个人情怀，情景交融，在白族文学史上占有重要地位。该诗刻于碑碣，流传至今，被后人称为"山花碑"，与"南诏德化碑"和"元世祖平云南碑"并称大理三大碑。诗文成功运用了"三七一五"的格律，为白族诗歌所特有，也被称为"山花体"。《词记山花·咏苍洱境》用汉字记白语，碑文若用白语吟咏，文辞优美，婉转动听。山花碑也是现存的白语古碑中最完整的一块，是研究西南民族历史、语言和文学的重要文献。山花碑原立于喜洲圣源寺观音阁内，现存于大理市博物馆。

（四）诗书画名僧担当

担当（1593—1673），原籍昆明晋宁，是明清之际的一位名僧，在当时以诗、书、画"三绝"闻名。早年在鸡足山出家，多游历，晚年常居苍山感通寺，大理可以说是他的第二故乡。担当的诗风格酷似唐代诗人王维，诗中有画，画中有诗，通俗畅达而富于风趣。画重写意，尤擅水墨山水。书法也很有名，擅草书、行书。他的诗书画在当年广为流传，也有不少书画流传至今，成为极具价值的文物珍品。鸡足山今存其字、画真迹。担当圆寂后葬于感通寺后山，其墓塔至今保存完好。

（五）近代学者赵藩

赵藩（1851—1927），剑川县人，近代著名诗人、学者、书法家。早年任职蜀中时曾为武侯祠撰联：能攻心，则反侧自消，从古知兵非好战；不审势，即宽严皆误，后来治蜀要深思。该联辩证地评价了诸葛亮，曾受到毛主席的称赞。赵藩的主要成就是诗文，内容多具有反帝、反封建、反军阀割据的民主进步倾向，在我国近代文坛有一定影响。其在书法上也卓有成就，现存昆明大观楼长联就是由他书写，深受后人赞誉。赵藩一生著述颇丰，晚年主持编纂的《云南丛书》集云南文献之大成，为收集、整理和保存云南地方文献做出了巨大贡献。

Section Three   A Prestigious State of Literature and Art

Dali is blessed with long-established cultural tradition and has always attached great importance to education. Generations of gifted talents have made brilliant literary and artistic achievements and therefore won Dali the reputation of "State of Literature".

Illustrated Story of Nanzhao

As a combination of painted and script scrolls, *Illustrated Story of Nanzhao* was created during the Nanzhao Kingdom in the second year of the Zhongxing reign period (898—902), hence also known as *Painting Scroll of Nanzhao* or *Painting Scroll of Zhongxing History*. The scroll illustrates the legend of Xinuluo establishing the Nanzhao Kingdom at the Weibaoshan Mountain, vividly and exquisitely depicting figures of all classes, including their attire and manners. It shows rich imagination and excellent artistic levels. It was preserved in the Qing royal court before being looted when the Eight-Nation Allied Force invaded Beijing. Only copies of the scroll can be found at home now while the original is kept abroad in Youlin Museum in Kyoto, Japan.

The Kingdom of Dali Buddhist Volume of Paintings

The Kingdom of Dali Buddhist Volume of Paintings was produced by Zhang Shengwen, an artist of the Dali kingdom. This long scroll of paintings, which describes both Buddhist stories and diplomatic affairs, is a great treasure of Buddhist images. Bearing a reputation as the "Treasure of the South", the scroll vividly portrays hundreds of figures in detailed strokes and dazzling colors. According to some scholars, the painting style of Zhang

Shengwen resembles that of the Dunhuang grotto murals, indicating that Dali was deeply influenced by the culture of the Central Plains at that time. The scroll was treasured by Emperor Qianlong in the Qing Dynasty. In 1944, it was exhibited in Chongqing and later brought to Taiwan, where it's presently housed in the Palace Museum in Taipei.

Yang Fu: Representative Poet of the Shanhua Style

Yang Fu was a poet, scholar, calligrapher and painter in the Ming Dynasty, living in reclusion all his life, with absolutely no intention of seeking official rank at all. Yang Fu's most famous poem *The Poem of Shanhua Ode to Cangshan Mountain and Erhai Lake* was written in Ancient Bai Script and of great importance in the history of Bai literature. This poem praises the stunning views of Cangshan Mountain and Erhai Lake and expresses his personal feelings at the same time. It's able to pass down to present time as the text was engraved on the Shanhua Tablet, one of the three greatest tablets in Dali. The other two are the Nanzhao Dehua Tablet and the Kublai Khan Quelling Yunnan Tablet respectively. Each verse of the poem contains three seven-word sentences and one five-word sentence, which is a typical Shanhua style unique to Bai poetry. Written in Ancient Bai Script, the poetry sounds beautiful when read in Bai language. As the most intact tablet in existence in Ancient Bai Script, the Shanhua Tablet is an important document for the historical, linguistic and literary study of ethnic groups in Southwest China. The tablet was first erected in the Guanyin Pavilion of Shengyuan Temple in Xizhou Town and has been moved to the Dali Municipal Museum.

Monk Dandang

Monk Dandang (1593—1673), born in Jinning, Kunming, lived in late Ming and early Qing dynasties and was famous for poetry, calligraphy and painting at his time. Becoming a monk at an early age at the Jizu Mountain of Dali, he traveled a lot when he was young and spent most of his twilight years in the Gantong Temple on Cangshan Mountain, so Dali was his second hometown. The style of Dandang's poetry is similar to that of Wang Wei, a widely known Tang-dynasty poet highly praised for putting painting into his poetry and poetry into his painting. Dandang was an expert in the ink-wash landscape paintings, and many of his works are free sketches. A good calligrapher as well, he's skillful in cursive and running scripts. People of his time scrambled to collect his works, many of which have passed down as valuable cultural relics. Today original handwriting and paintings of Dandang can be found in Jizu Mountain, and behind the Gantong Temple stands the well-preserved tomb of him.

Zhao Fan: a Scholar of Modern Times

Zhao Fan (1851—1927), born in Jianchuan County, was a famous poet, scholar and calligrapher in modern times. While holding office in Sichuan Province, Zhao composed a couplet for the Wuhou Temple, which objectively appraised Zhuge Liang and won high praise from Chairman Mao. He is particularly known in modern literary world for his poems, most of which embody a democratic progressive tendency of anti-imperialism, anti-feudalism and anti-warlordism. In terms of calligraphy, where Zhao was also accomplished, the Lengthened Couplet of Daguan Pavilion in Kunming was handwritten by him and highly praised by later generations. Among the many works by Zhao Fan, *Collected Works of Yunnan*, compiled in his later years, is the greatest collection of documents in Yunnan and a valuable contribution to the collection and preservation of local documents.

Think and Discuss:

　　由于历史原因,我国许多优秀的国宝文物流失海外,如《南诏图传》至今仍流落日本,国内民众难睹其真容,令人深感遗憾。也有一些失落文物通过社会各界的努力得以重回祖国怀抱。对此你有何感想?你知道哪些失落文物回归祖国的事例?

第四节　精雕细琢　匠心大理

民间手工艺术历来是大理的骄傲。剑川木雕的精湛工艺、鹤庆的银器加工、大理石制作技艺等都被列入各级非物质文化遗产名录，组成了一道道亮丽的风景线。

（一）剑川木雕工艺

木雕是大理剑川县群众世代相传的一种传统技艺，已有一千多年的历史。从古至今，剑川木匠们走南闯北，名扬四方。北京的故宫、承德的避暑山庄和昆明的金马碧鸡坊等著名古建筑上都有剑川木雕的精湛呈现。中华人民共和国成立后，剑川木雕有了很大的发展。首都人民大会堂、民族文化宫等重要建筑都饰有剑川木雕。

剑川县素称"木雕之乡"，木雕图案主要有人物、动物和花卉三大类，多为寓意吉祥富贵的传统题材，用以装饰门窗、家具等，具有浓郁的地方特色。剑川木雕产品选用优质的红木、西南桦、缅甸红木和天然植物漆，具有很高的实用价值、工艺价值和收藏价值。2011年5月，剑川木雕被国务院列入第三批国家级非物质文化遗产项目。

剑川木雕兼南北之长，融粗犷豪放和细腻精巧于一身，成为全国木雕重要派别之一。它与剑川石钟山石窟一脉相承，被誉为"滇中双绝"。

（二）鹤庆银器锻制技艺

鹤庆银器锻制技艺传承历史久远，是一项独具特色的传统手工艺。2014年11月，被国务院列入第四批国家级非物质文化遗产名录。

作为鹤庆手工银器产业核心的新华村位于鹤庆县草海镇西北的凤凰山脚。这里是茶马古道的必经之地，也是一个"小锤敲过一千年"的古老村寨。

据史料记载，早在唐朝南诏时期新华村就有了以银器为主的金属手工艺品加工制作技艺。这里出产的银器曾沿着茶马古道大量输送到尼泊尔、印度等国。

近年来，鹤庆银器加工逐渐走向多元化、规模化，形成了以新华村为核心、辐射周边多个村寨的庞大加工产业群。初步统计，仅新华村年加工纯银就达近百吨，产品远销全国各地及美国、日本、印度、马来西亚、尼泊尔、泰国、巴基斯坦等国家。新华村也因银器锻制工艺成为鹤庆的一张文化名片，有"银都水乡"之美誉。

（三）大理石制作技艺

大理石是大理市境内的特有石种，主要产于苍山，有彩花石、水花石、苍白玉三个品种，有红、紫、绿、黑、灰、白等天然花纹，不仅是一种天然的建筑装饰材料，也是制作各式手工艺品的上等石材。

大理石制作技艺历史悠久，是大理地区特有的传统工艺，现在大理市境内的大理镇、银桥镇等地都有众多的大理石厂。2009年10月，大理石制作技艺被列入省级非物质文化遗产名录。

由于大理石的颜色、花纹得天独厚，因此加工大理石时，常根据不同的石质纹理和颜色将大理石制成如花盆、屏风、花瓶、笔筒等小型工艺品或如餐桌、茶几、桌椅等家具及家居用品，大的还可用于各类雕塑、石雕作品及各种建筑用材。由于其用途广泛且风格独特，2012年10月，大理市人民政府正式把大理石确定为市石。

Section Four Exquisite Craftsmanship

Traditional handicrafts have always been Dali's pride. The wood carving in Jianchuan, silver processing skills in Heqing and marble making skills in

Dali are typical representatives and listed in the Intangible Cultural Heritage List at different levels.

Jianchuan Wood Carving

In Jianchuan County, wood carving is a traditional handicraft technique with more than a millennium years of history. Local craftsmen have inherited and passed on their skills from generation to generation. Since ancient times, the carpenters in Jianchuan traveled across the country and became renowned for their skills. Many woodworking parts of the Forbidden City in Beijing, the Mountain Resort in Chengde, the Jinma Biji Square in Kunming and other famous ancient buildings are the handiwork of Jianchuan carpenters and an exquisite presentation of Jianchuan wood carving. After the founding of the People's Republic of China, Jianchuan wood carving had a profound development. The Great Hall of the People, the Cultural Palace of Nationalities and other important buildings in Beijing are decorated with Jianchuan wood carvings.

Jianchuan County is known as the "Hometown of Woodcarving". The carvings feature patterns of figures, animals and flowers, most of which are of traditional themes implying auspiciousness and wealth. They are used to decorate doors, windows and furniture, embodying unique characteristics. Craftsmen choose high-quality mahogany, southwest birch, Myanmar redwood and natural plant lacquer as raw materials, thus giving the products practical use and artistic value, and making them worthy of collection. In May 2011, Jianchuan woodcarving was placed in the third batch of the National Intangible Cultural Heritage List by the State Council.

Jianchuan wood carving, a combination of boldness and exquisiteness, collects the essence of both the northern and southern wood carving styles and becomes one of the major schools of wood carving in China. Along with the Shizhongshan Grottoes located in Jianchuan County, it was hailed as the "Two Wonders of Central Yunnan".

Heqing Silver Making

As a traditional handicraft with a long history, Heqing silver making was listed in the fourth batch of National Intangible Cultural Heritage List by the State Council in November 2014.

Xinhua Village, the center of Heqing silver-making industry, is located at the foot of Fenghuang Mountain in the northwest of Caohai Town, Heqing County. Sitting on the ancient Tea-Horse Road, this is an old village where "small hammers have been hammered for a thousand years". According to historical records, the production of metal (especially silver) handicrafts in Xinhua Village dates back as early as the Tang Dynasty. Silver products here were transported in large quantities to Nepal, India and other countries by way of the Tea-Horse Road.

In recent years, silver processing in Heqing has diversified and scaled up, gradually forming a huge industrial group with Xinhua Village in the center and incorporating multiple surrounding villages. According to rough statistics, the annual processing of silver in Xinhua Village alone reaches nearly 100 tons, and the products are exported to all over the country, the United States, Japan, India, Malaysia, Nepal, Thailand, Pakistan and other countries. Xinhua Village has become a cultural card of Heqing and wins the reputation of "Village of Silver and Water".

Dali Marble Processing Skills

Marble, known as Dali Stone (Dali Shi) in Chinese, is an indigenous product mainly quarried in the Cangshan mountain range. This kind of stone has unique veins of different color, including red, purple, green, black, gray and white. Dali marble appears in three major varieties: Caihua, Shuihua and Cangbaiyu. It's a fine natural material for architectural decoration and handicraft making.

The traditional skill of marble making has a long history in Dali. There are many marble factories in Dali Town, Yinqiao Town and other places in Dali City. In October 2009, marble-making skills were included in the Provincial Intangible Cultural Heritage List.

Depending on its colors and patterns, Dali marble is processed into different things: small handicrafts like flowerpots, screens, vases and pen containers, or furniture like dining tables, tea tables, desks and chairs. Big ones can be used for sculptures, stone carvings and building materials. Due to its wide use and unique style, Dali marble was officially designated as the City Stone by the municipal government in October 2012.

> **Think and Discuss:**
> 在快节奏的现代生活中，许多传统手工艺日渐没落，陷入无人传承的窘境。你认为保护传统手工艺的意义是什么？请为传统手工艺的传承和发扬献计献策。

第五节　品茗论道　茶艺大理

大理地区自古以来就有客来敬茶、以茶会友的习俗，并形成了自己的独特茶道。

三道茶是大理地区的传统茶道，是一种将茶叶精心烘烤，分道加入各种辅料，然后依次饮用的品茶方式。第一道为苦茶，将茶叶放入特制的小陶罐置于炭火上烘烤，待茶叶微黄、清香四溢时冲入少许沸水即成清苦之茶。头道茶茶味苦涩，寓意人生首先要敢于吃苦。第二道为甜茶，在苦茶内加入乳扇、核桃仁、红糖等佐料，香甜可口，意指幸福生活来之不易。第三道为回味茶，苦茶内加入少许蜂蜜、花椒、生姜、桂皮而成，饮后回味无穷。此道茶寓意人生要常有反思，有温故知新的含义。

三道茶暗合"一苦二甜三回味"的人生哲理，是借茶喻世的独有茶道，饮茶的同时还可以尽情享受茶礼、观赏茶艺、体悟人生。其起源于南诏时期，传承至今已有千余年。历史上只有在节日或某些特定场合才用三道茶待客。近年来，当地文旅部门将三道茶开发为集音乐、歌舞与品茗为一体的特色茶道，深受海内外人士喜爱。

Section Five　The Three-Course Tea Ceremony

Dali people have a long tradition of entertaining guests and friends with tea and have developed their own special tea ceremony.

The so-called Three-Course Tea is long practiced by Dali people. They bake the tea leaves, add various ingredients in each course and drink them one by one. The first course of tea tastes bitter. They put some tea leaves into a small clay pot, bake them on the fire and pour boiling water when the tea leaves turn yellowish and give off fragrance. The bitter first cup of tea has a deeper symbolic meaning: one has to overcome difficulties before making great achievements. The second course is sweet, made by adding rushan (milk fan, a local diary snack), walnuts, brown sugar and other ingredients into the bitter tea. It implies that happiness will finally come after all the hardships. The third course is for aftertaste, served with honey, pepper, ginger and cinnamon. It suggests one can recall both bitterness and sweetness after experiencing all pains and pleasures of life.

This meaningful tea ceremony allows you to enjoy the tea and understand life philosophy in the meantime. It has a history of more than one thousand years and can be traced back to the Nanzhao Kingdom. In the past, the Three-Course Tea was served only on festivals or special occasions. In recent years, however, local governments have developed it into a featured tea ceremony: a combination of ethnic music, singing, dancing and tea drinking, which is warmly received by tourists at home and abroad.

Think and Discuss:
　　三道茶中蕴含着先苦后甜的人生体悟，你赞同这种人生哲学吗？有人更倾向于先甜后苦，你怎么看？

第六节 古朴民居 乡愁大理

传统风貌保持良好的民居最能唤起人们内心的乡愁。国家主席习近平在大理古生村视察时就曾高度评价当地的民居建筑："这里环境整洁，又保持着古朴形态，这样的庭院比西式洋房好，记得住乡愁。"

大理地区的传统民居多为石木建筑。擅于用当地丰富的石料来修建房屋，是大理地区建筑的主要特征。现在的民居建筑依然保持着这一传统。

大理民居以"坊"为基本建筑单元，以"三坊一照壁""四合五天井"为代表性格局。所谓"三坊一照壁"是指由三坊住房与一堵照壁围成的院落，正对照壁的一坊为主房，其余两幢为厢房。照壁可将日光反射进主房，同时能起到遮挡和保护隐私的作用。"四合五天井"是指由四坊住房组成的建筑单元。四坊中间合围成一个大院子（天井），四角两两相交而不相连，又形成四个小院子，从而构成"四合五天井"的格局。

大理民居特别重视门楼、照壁、山墙的建造。这些地方常有雕刻、绘画等装饰，往往十分精致华丽，是大理民居的一大特色。照壁正中常以白灰粉刷，上书四字题词。题字内容常因屋主姓氏而各不相同，如杨姓题"清白传家"，张姓题"百忍家风"等。各姓氏照壁题字都有典故，互相不能混淆。

大理民间崇尚白色，其建筑外墙均以白色为主调。白墙青瓦，典雅大方。大理民居十分讲究住宅环境的优雅整洁。院子常以石板铺就，照壁前多有花坛，院内广植花木。大理民居反映着当地人民对自然美、生活美的向往和追求，也是人与自然和谐相处的真实写照。喜洲民居作为大理民居建筑的典型代表已被列入国家级文物保护单位。

Section Six   Traditional Folk Architecture

Folk houses full of traditional flavor help preserve a deep memory of the countryside. While visiting Gusheng Village in Dali, President Xi Jinping spoke highly of the local residences. He remarked, "Not only is this place clean and tidy, it also preserves a plain and simple style. I think this kind of courtyard is better than a Western style house, because it carries a sense of nostalgia for the countryside."

Traditional Dali houses are mostly built of stone and wood. The use of local stone materials is a leading architectural feature inherited by contemporary houses in Dali.

There are two basic types of residences in Dali. The "three rooms and one screen wall" type has one main room, two long side rooms and a "screen wall" on the fourth side facing the main room. The screen wall, or "shining wall", is designed to reflect light back into the main room and provide a little extra privacy. The "four houses and five courtyards" type is made up of four long rooms arranged in a square shape. In each of the square's four corners there is a mini courtyard and the space in the middle makes up the fifth, largest courtyard.

The gates and walls are often exquisitely decorated with sculptures and paintings, which is a special charm of Dali dwellings. The shinning wall is normally painted white with slaked lime and inscribed with a meaningful Chinese proverb consisting of four characters. One can always tell if a mansion belongs to a specific clan according to the slogan on the shining wall. As an example, the Yang family's wall reads "Generations of Righteousness" while Zhang's wall is inscribed with "A Tradition of Tolerance". There are stories behind these family slogans, which shouldn't be confused with one another.

Dali people love white color. The walls of their houses are all painted white and covered with black tiles. They pay much attention to their living environment. The courtyard is often covered by flagstones. There are usually flower beds in front of the screen wall, and flowers and trees are widely planted in their courtyards. Dali homes speak of people's pursuit of beauty and the harmony between man and nature. Xizhou folk architecture, a typical representative of folk residences in Dali, has been listed as a major historical and cultural site protected at the national level.

Think and Discuss:

有人说白族照壁是有生命、会说话的建筑，照壁题字彰显的"家风"其实就是各家最看重的家庭教育理念。中华民族有重视家教的文化传统。2022年1月1日，我国首部家庭教育领域的专门立法《中华人民共和国家庭教育促进法》正式实施，标志着家庭教育将由传统"家事"上升为新时代"国事"。对此你有什么看法？在当今时代背景下，你认为正确的家庭教育观应该是什么？

第七节　苍洱摇篮　宜居大理

近年来，大理州始终坚持生态优先发展战略，秉持"绿水青山就是金山银山"的坚定信念，不断加强生态文明建设，着力打造生态宜居新大理。这一发展思路集中体现在洱海的治理与保护上。

"苍山不墨千秋画，洱海无弦万古情"是大理美景的写照。然而，如此美景也曾因严重的水污染而失去光芒。洱海是云南省第二大淡水湖，也是大理各族人民赖以生存和发展的"母亲湖"。然而，随着旅游业的兴起和城市化进程的加快，洱海水质急剧下降，蓝藻大面积暴发，水污染问题一度非常突出。2015年1月，习近平主席在大理视察时提出，一定要把洱海保护好，一场史无前例的保护与治理攻坚战由此打响。

为了保护好大理人民的"母亲湖"，从当地政府到流域内群众都以"壮士断腕"的决心，对发展模式和生产方式做出了巨大改变，为湖泊保护让路。如拆除违章建筑、腾退近岸土地、进一步规范餐饮客栈经营行为。从2019年起当地政府对洱海实行全年封湖禁渔。当地百姓放弃了需要使用大量农药和肥料的大蒜种植传统，改种水稻、烤烟等低肥水作物。总之，最大限度减少人类活动对湖体的影响，努力在洱海流域内实现人与自然和谐共生。"像保护眼睛一样保护洱海""洱海清、大理兴"的治理理念深入人心。

此外，全长129千米的洱海生态廊道建成后为洱海治理筑起了一道绿色屏障，也给人民群众创造了一个生态宜居、环境优美的生活和生态空间，让广大人民群众也能共享洱海保护治理的成果，从而进一步提高全民环境保护意识。

苍山之美，在其雄浑巍峨；洱海之美，在其干净清澈。通过大理全州

上下的共同努力，洱海水体生态功能不断得到恢复，水质不断提升，一度消失的"水质风向标"海菜花重现洱海。苍洱风光，再度明媚。目前，大理洱海是全国城市近郊保护最好的湖泊之一。山、海、岛、湿地等自然地理地貌在大理州内和谐共存，为创建宜居大理提供了无可取代的天然条件。

Section Seven   An Ecologically Livable City

In recent years, Dali has been prioritizing ecological and environmental protection. Under the firm belief that "lucid waters and lush mountains are invaluable assets", Dali is collecting all efforts to build an ecologically livable city, as clearly reflected in the restoration and conservation of Erhai Lake.

"With no ink, the Cangshan Mountains paint a picture of timeless grandeur; with no strings, the Erhai Lake plucks a melody of incredible harmony." This couplet deftly evokes the beauty of the Cangshan Mountains and Erhai Lake. However, there was a time when this beauty was unable to shine through because of the stain of water pollution. Erhai Lake is the second largest fresh water lake in Yunnan Province and the "mother lake" on which local people rely for their survival. However, the booming tourism, coupled with rapid urbanization, took its toll on the lake, causing water quality degradation and toxic blue-green algae blooms. During an inspection tour of Yunnan in January 2015, President Xi Jinping visited the lake and instructed that Erhai Lake must be protected. In response to President Xi Jinping's call, a series of ecological projects were launched to prevent and control pollution and restore the environment of Erhai Lake.

Both local governments and the people have made great efforts and sacrifices to make way for the restoration projects. They've adjusted their industrial structure and turned it to a green development model. Initiatives included demolishing illegal constructions around the lake, restoring the wetlands and regulating the operation of restaurants and guesthouses. The government has implemented a total ban on fishing in the lake since 2019. All fishing activities were banned all year round. Local farmers have stopped growing garlic, which entails the use of large amounts of pesticides and chemical fertilizers, and switched to rice, tobacco and other replacement crops that use less water and fertilizer. In a word, they endeavor to minimize the impact of human activities on the lake and strive to achieve harmonious coexistence between man and nature. "Protect the Erhai Lake like protecting our own eyes." "A prosperous Dali calls for a clear Erhai Lake." Such slogans have taken root in local people's hearts.

Meanwhile, the 129-kilometer Erhai Lake Ecological Corridor not only functions as an environmental protection system but also offers an ecologically livable space and enjoyable environment for locals, so that the majority of people can benefit from protecting the lake and further improve their awareness of environmental protection.

Cangshan Mountain is cherished for its loftiness while Erhai Lake for its lucidity. Through the joint efforts of the government and the public, the water quality of Erhai Lake has been significantly improved in recent years, which brings back the once-vanished ottelia acuminate, an aquatic plant species known as the "touchstone of water quality". The plateau lake regains its lost luster. Erhai Lake remains one of the best protected lakes on the city outskirts in China. The mountains and lakes, along with islands, wetlands and other natural landforms, provide irreplaceable preconditions for building a livable Dali.

Think and Discuss:

在漫长而艰难的治理过程中，洱海流域的人民做出了巨大的牺牲，当地的经济发展也受到了影响。你认为该如何平衡经济发展与生态保护的关系？如何才能真正实现人与自然和谐共生？

第四章　西双版纳篇
Chapter IV　Xishuangbanna

第一节　勐巴拉娜西，理想而神奇的乐土

西双版纳，古代傣语为"勐巴拉娜西"，意思是"理想而神奇的乐土"，以神奇的热带雨林自然景观闻名于世。西双版纳位于云南省的南部，它的首府是景洪市，北边紧挨普洱市，东南与老挝接壤，西南与缅甸相邻。西双版纳离泰国也很近，从景洪市的中缅边境出发，穿过缅甸就可以到达泰国北部的边境，最近的距离大概只有180千米。

西双版纳地形的整体特点是北边高，南边低，地势由北向南倾斜。州内海拔最高为2429米，海拔最低点为477米，全州大部分地区海拔均在1500米以下，地形呈现中间低，四周高。整个州主要为山地，约占总面积的95%。山与山之间分布着许多当地人称之为"坝子"的盆地，约占全州面积的5%。西双版纳的主要河流是澜沧江，澜沧江纵贯西双版纳全境并流到境外，境外段被称为湄公河。在傣语、老挝语及泰语中，"湄"意为母亲，"公"的意思是河流，"湄公河"也就是母亲河。澜沧江-湄公河全长四千九百多千米，流经老挝、缅甸、泰国、柬埔寨，最后从越南的胡志明市注入太平洋。作为国际性河流，其流经国家众多，流域面积广，是沿岸各国人民经济和文化的走廊，因此有"东方多瑙河"的美誉。

西双版纳的热带雨林是高纬度、高海拔地带保存最完整的热带雨林。

珍稀动物、植物和整个森林生态系统都是无价之宝，因为它是世界上唯一保存完好、连片大面积的热带森林，还有全球绝无仅有的植物垂直分布"倒置"现象，被誉为地球的一大自然奇观。

Section One Mengbalanaxi, an Ideal and Magical Paradise

Xishuangbanna, which was referred to as "Mengbalanaxi" in the ancient Dai language, meaning "an ideal and magical paradise", is famous for its miraculous natural landscape of tropical rainforests. Xishuangbanna is located in the south of Yunnan Province and its capital is Jinghong City. With Pu'er City to the north, it is bordered on the southeast by Laos and on the southwest by Myanmar. Xishuangbanna is also close to Thailand. Starting from the China-Myanmar border in Jinghong City and then passing through Myanmar, one can reach the northern border of Thailand. The shortest distance is only about 180 kilometers.

The main geographical feature of Xishuangbanna is that highlands are in the north while lowlands in the south, so the terrain tilts from north to south. The highest point of elevation in the prefecture is 2,429 meters above the sea level, while the lowest altitude is 477 meters. The altitudes of most parts are below 1,500 meters above sea level. The central lowlands are surrounded by the highlands. The prefecture is mountainous, with mountainous lands accounting for about 95% of the total landmass. There are many basins called "Bazi" by the locals among the mountains, occupying about 5% of the whole prefecture. The most important river is Lancang River, which runs through the whole territory of Xishuangbanna and flows out of the country. The overseas section is known as Mekong River. In Dai, Lao and Thai, "Me" means mother and "Kong" means river, therefore, "Mekong" denotes "the Mother River". The Lancang-Mekong River, with a total length of more than 4,900 kilometers, flows through Laos, Myanmar, Thailand and Cambodia, and finally runs into the Pacific Ocean from Ho Chi Minh City in Vietnam. Flowing through many countries and having a wide drainage area, the international river serves as an economic and cultural corridor for the people of the coastal countries and is honorifically regarded as "The Oriental Danube".

The tropical rainforest in Xishuangbanna is the most intact one in high latitudes and altitudes. Rare animals, plants and the whole forest ecosystem of it are all priceless, because it is the only well-preserved tropical forest with a large area in the world. Its unique "inverted" phenomenon of vertical distribution of plants is known as a natural wonder of the earth.

Think and Discuss:

为什么热带雨林被称为"地球之肺"？它对全球生态系统有什么重要的意义？

第二节　幸福在哪里？西双版纳告诉你

西双版纳因地理位置的特殊性，温度、湿度适宜，植被覆盖率高，物产丰富，人民安居乐业，幸福指数位居全国前列。在 2021 年"中国十大环境舒适之城"评选中，西双版纳空气清新指数、水质清净指数、绿化清秀指数等评价位居第一。此外，这里消费水平不是很高，生活节奏也比较慢，人也非常随和，因此，不仅适合长期居住，也是短期出行的最佳旅游目的地之一。

（一）气候宜人　舒适宜居

西双版纳处于热带北部边缘，北边有哀牢山和无量山作为屏障阻挡了南下的寒流。在南面，由于东西两边靠近印度洋和孟加拉湾，夏季受到印度洋季风和太平洋气流的影响，形成了高温多雨、干湿季分明而四季不明显的气候特点。西双版纳终年温差较小，一般在 18~22℃。一般来说，干季从 11 月开始持续到次年的 4 月，云和雨少，但光照很强，这使得冬天的温度会明显提高；此外，浓重的雾和露又能弥补降水量的不足。湿季从 5 月到 10 月，在这期间，云雨多，风速小，日照少，使得气温偏高且空气湿度大。总的来说，西双版纳具有常年温润、光照充足、降水丰沛、静风少寒、干湿季分明的气候特点，是全国稀缺的一级舒适避寒地。丰厚的森林资源也带来了不一样的呼吸感受，高浓度的大气负氧离子让其有了"全球绿肺"之称。

竹楼曾是西双版纳民居的标志，最早的竹楼全部是用竹子建造的，下层储藏，上层居住，但不够结实，很容易坏，每年雨季后都需要修整。经济的发展，科技的进步，悄悄改变着建筑的材料和外貌。现在，旧式的竹楼已经很少见，在一些古老的村落里可以看见改造后的新式竹楼。城市里，遍地都是钢筋混凝土的高楼大厦。如西双版纳的景洪市就是高楼林立，车水马龙。尽管如此，由于其丰富的植物资源和特色的城市园林景观，人们仍可以感受到"城在林中，居在园中"，加上房价比起很多热门城市并不算高，因此，吸引了越来越多的人在此买房、安家。

（二）另类美食

西双版纳的当地食物独具特色，自成体系，基本的烹饪方法是烤、炸、蒸、剁、腌，很少炒菜；味道以酸辣见长。人们认为，吃酸的有助消化，多吃酸的可以消暑解热。吃辣的可以增进食欲，预防伤风感冒。

舂鸡脚

舂（chōng），是用杵在钵里把东西捣碎的意思。将用清水煮熟的鸡爪连同小米辣等各种香料一起捣碎，再加入盐巴、柠檬汁等和黄瓜、胡萝卜丝一起拌匀，就做成了酸辣爽口的舂鸡脚。西双版纳人民喜好酸辣的食物，凉拌类食品品种繁多，舂鸡脚是其中的一道热门菜肴。在西双版纳，万物皆可舂，除了舂鸡脚外，还有舂黄瓜、舂猪皮、舂米线和舂方便面等。

傣味烧烤

傣味烧烤品种丰富，除了各种肉制品、菌类，还有各式各样当地大山中的野生食材，如野生小苦瓜、野茄子、芭蕉花等。比较特别的烧烤是烤鸡、烤鱼、烤鹌鹑、烤五花肉等，烤串都是用竹片夹住，个头相当大，分量十足，而且每种烤肉串基本都会使用香茅草。香茅草是生长在亚热带的一种香料，天然带柠檬香味，不仅可以去腥，还可以使烤出来的肉串更香。

香茅草烤鱼是最能代表傣味烧烤的一道菜肴。它是用青竹片夹住当地生长的罗非鱼，用明火烤，既有烤肉的香，又有竹的清香，更有香茅奇特的香味，吃起来鲜嫩奇香。在西双版纳的烧烤摊，还能吃到各种各样的油炸虫子，如油炸竹虫、蝗虫等。竹虫生长在野生毛竹内，吃新鲜的竹子，当地人从森林中砍回毛竹，打开竹筒就可以取出竹虫，油炸后配上椒盐，味道油而不腻，口感独特。每年雨季，在本地菜馆都可以品尝到这类特色菜肴。

手抓饭和竹筒饭

手抓饭也被称为"绿叶宴"，是西双版纳的特色美食。桌子上先铺一层洗干净的芭蕉叶，然后将米饭放在中间，有大米饭、紫米饭等，米饭上用各种食材加以装饰。米饭四周用各种菜肴和蘸料摆成一圈，有烤鱼、烤五花肉、油炸猪皮、柠檬鸡、牛干巴等。按传统，吃手抓饭是不用筷子和碗的，直接用手抓了吃。炭火是西双版纳人民在烹调上的好帮手，竹筒饭也是经过炭火烤制而成的，用当地特产的香竹装入紫糯米、花生米进行烘烤，香竹的天然气息融入了糯米的清香，这一道菜也是当地美食的代表。

泡鲁达和老挝冰咖啡

在西双版纳的很多餐厅里，都会看到非常著名的小吃——泡鲁达，它是用西米、木瓜冻、缅甸炼乳、特制奶油面包干、新鲜椰丝加上碎冰块制作而成。做好的泡鲁达，奶油面包干泡在奶香浓郁的冰水中，香甜扑鼻，非常爽口。

近几年，在景洪的大街小巷随处可见售卖老挝冰咖啡的小店或摊位。老挝冰咖啡是在制作好的黑咖啡中加入炼乳，并直接装在铺满冰块的塑料袋里，然后将塑料袋放进各种图案的印花纸袋里，喝的时候，直接用吸管戳破塑料袋即可。炎炎夏日，一杯浓香醇厚的冰镇咖啡可以解暑散热，消除疲劳。

（三）奇趣民俗

丢包，是欢度新年佳节的重要活动之一。参加丢包活动的人，都是未婚的青年男女。想要寻找伴侣的姑娘和小伙子，首先在空地上分开站成两队，经过短暂的观察，姑娘们首先一字儿排开，手持用各色花布和丝线精心缝制的花包，选中了自己心仪的人后，便把布包向对方扔过去，如对方接着，就意味着男方对女方也有意。

泼水节是一年中最盛大的传统节日，它的傣语意思是六月新年，象征着"最美好的日子"。过去，通常是在公历的4月中旬举行，为期3天，现已固定在公历4月13至15日举行。前两天是送旧，最后一天迎新。节日期间，人们相互泼水祝福，并举行拜佛、赛龙舟、放高升和点孔明灯等活动。每年泼水节的时候，都要在澜沧江举行声势浩大的龙舟赛，现在澜沧江的龙舟赛已是西双版纳最隆重的盛事之一。泼水节是展现当地传统文化的综合平台，也是加强全州各族人民大团结的重要纽带，对促进西双版纳与东南亚各国友好的合作交流、全州社会经济文化的发展都起到了积极作用。

象脚鼓舞是在西双版纳流传最广的男性舞蹈，还被列入了国家级保护名录。之所以叫象脚鼓舞，是因为在跳舞的时候，每个舞者都要挎着形状像大象脚的鼓。象脚鼓用芒果树或木棉树干挖空，蒙上牛皮制成。象脚鼓舞的特点是动作节奏性强，一边用手敲打鼓，一边还要用脚踢踏地面，同时胸部要拱缩、肩部要耸动。它是重要节日当中必不可少的一项活动，因此，哪里有象脚鼓声，哪里就有欢乐的人群。

Section Two　　Where Is Happiness? You Can Find it in Xishuangbanna

Xishuangbanna, with its special geographical location, suitable temperature and humidity, high vegetation coverage rate, rich products and people living and working in peace and contentment, ranks among the top in China in terms of happiness index. In the selection of "China's Top 10 Environmentally Comfortable Cities" in 2021, Xishuangbanna ranked first in the evaluation of air, water, greening areas and so on. In addition, the consumption level here is not very high, the pace of life is relatively slow, and people here are easygoing, making it not only suitable for long-term living but also one of the best tourist destinations for short-term trips.

The Pleasant Climate and Livable Environment

Xishuangbanna is located on the northern edge of the tropics, with Ailao Mountain and Wuliang Mountain in the north blocking the cold current going south. In the south, the east side is close to the Indian Ocean and the west adjacent to the Bay of Bengal, so the climate will be affected by the Indian Ocean monsoon and Pacific airflow in summer, with the characteristics of high temperatures, raininess and dry or wet season instead of four distinctive seasons. The annual average temperature varies slightly all year round, which is generally between 18 and 22 degrees Celsius. Generally speaking, the dry season lasts from November to April of the next year with few clouds and little rain, but the light is strong, causing a significant rise in the temperature in winter. On the other hand, heavy fog and dew can make up for the lack of precipitation. The wet season is from May to October, during which there are a lot of clouds, rain and gentle breezes but less sunshine, resulting in higher temperatures and air humidity. In general, Xishuangbanna is characterized by warm weather all year round, sufficient light, abundant precipitation, less cold and wind and distinct wet and dry seasons, which makes it a rare class-A resort to spend the winter. Rich forest resources also contribute to refreshing air, with the high concentration of negative oxygen ion, Xishuangbanna is honored as the "Global Green Lung".

Bamboo buildings used to be the symbol of residential houses in Xishuangbanna. The earliest bamboo buildings were all built of bamboo, with the lower floor for storage and the upper floor for living. However, they were not strong enough and were easily broken, so they needed to be repaired every year after the rainy season. The development of economy and the progress of science and technology have quietly changed the construction materials and appearances of buildings. Nowadays, the old bamboo buildings are rare. Only in some ancient villages can you still see the renovated bamboo buildings. In the cities, there are skyscrapers of steel and concrete everywhere. For example, Jinghong City in Xishuangbanna is now full of tall buildings and heavy traffic, however, people can still feel that their city is in the forest, and they are living in the garden because of its rich plant resources and characteristic urban landscape. In addition, housing prices here are not that high compared with many popular cities, so more and more people are attracted to buy houses and settle down here.

Special Cuisine

The local cuisine of Xishuangbanna is self-contained with its unique flavor. The common cooking methods include baking, frying, steaming, chopping and pickling, while stir-frying is seldom seen. The cuisine is characterized by its sour and spicy flavors for people believe that sour food can promote digestion, relieve summer heat, quench thirst and eating more spicy food boosts appetite and prevents colds.

Smashed Chicken Feet

"Chong" means smashing things in a bowl with a pestle. The chicken feet cooked in plain water are crushed together with various spices like millet, and then mixed with salt, lemon juice, cucumber and shredded carrot. People in Xishuangbanna like spicy and sour foods, and there are many kinds of cold dishes, among which smashed chicken feet is one of the most popular. In

Xishuangbanna, many ingredients can be smashed and seasoned. Apart from smashed chicken feet, there are smashed cucumber, smashed pig skin, smashed rice noodles, and even smashed instant noodles.

Dai Barbecue

Dai barbecue is rich in varieties. In addition to all kinds of meat and fungi, there are a wide variety of edible wild herbs picked in local mountains, such as wild bitter gourd, eggplant and banana flower. The grilled chicken, fish, quail and pork belly are quite special, since they are all clamped with bamboo pieces and seasoned with fragrant thatch, with a large portion. Fragrant thatch is a spice growing in the subtropical zone, and its natural lemon flavor can not only remove the fishy smell, but also make the roasted meat tastier.

Grilled fish with fragrant thatch is typical of Dai barbecue. Locally grown tilapia clamped by green bamboo slices are grilled over an open fire. Mingled with the aroma of meat, bamboo and fragrant thatch, the fish tastes fresh and tender. All kinds of fried insects are also available at the barbecue stands in Xishuangbanna, such as fried bamboo insects, locusts and so on. Bamboo insects grow in wild moso bamboo and feed on fresh bamboo. Local people cut down moso bamboo, split the tube and take out the insects. The fried bamboo insects with pepper and salt taste oily but not greasy and this unique cuisine is available in local restaurants in every rainy season.

Hand Pilaf and Bamboo Tube Rice

The Dai pilaf is a characteristic local food in Xishuangbanna, known as "green leaf banquet". After a layer of washed banana leaves are spread on the table, the cooked rice is then put in the middle, including white rice, purple rice and so on. Decorated with various ingredients, the rice is surrounded by a circle of different dishes and cuisines, such as roast fish, roast pork belly, fried pig skin, lemon chicken and dried beef. Traditionally, chopsticks and bowls are not needed and people just grab the dishes by hand. Charcoal fire is a good helper for people in Xishuangbanna in cooking, and bamboo tube rice, the representative of local cuisine, is also baked by charcoal fire. As local bamboo tubes filled with purple glutinous rice and peanuts are baked on the fire, the natural flavor of the bamboo integrates with the fragrance of rice.

Falooda and Lao Iced Coffee

As a famous snack, Falooda is commonly seen in many restaurants in Xishuangbanna. It is made of sago, papaya jelly, Myanmar condensed milk, special-made rusks, shredded coconut and crushed ice. The rusks soaked in ice water have a strong milk aroma and taste sweet and refreshing.

In recent years, small shops or stands selling Lao iced coffee can be seen everywhere in the streets and alleys of Jinghong City. Lao iced coffee is made by adding condensed milk to the black coffee, and then putting the mixture directly into a plastic bag with its bottom covered with ice. Next, the plastic bag is put into a printed paper bag with various patterns or pictures. When drinking, one can directly break the plastic bag with a straw. In hot summer, a bag of mellow iced coffee can help to relieve heat and fatigue.

Interesting Folk Customs

Pouch throwing is one of the important activities to celebrate the New Year. Those who take part in the activity are all single young men and women. Girls and boys who want to find a partner stand in two teams in the open air. After a short-time observation, the girls first line up, each girl holding a pouch delicately sewn with colorful cloth and silk threads. Once she selects the boy she likes, she throws her pouch to him. If the boy catches the pouch, it means he is also fond of her.

The Water-splashing Festival is the biggest traditional festival in a whole year. It means "June New Year" in the Dai language and symbolizes the "best days". In the past, it was usually celebrated in the middle of April of the Gregorian calendar and lasted for three days while it is now fixed to be held from April 13 to 15. In the first two days, people are supposed to ring out the Old Year, while they spend the last day celebrating the New Year. During the festival, people sprinkle water onto others to give best wishes, and also hold activities like worshipping Buddha, dragon boat racing, and lighting Kongming lanterns. In every Water-splashing Festival, a grand dragon boat race is held in the Lancang River, which is one of the most spectacular events in Xishuangbanna. The Water-splashing Festival is not only a comprehensive platform to display the traditional local culture, but also an important link to strengthen the unity of people of all ethnic groups in the prefecture. Besides, it has also played a positive role in the cooperation and exchanges between Xishuangbanna and Southeast Asian countries and in the social, economic and cultural development of the prefecture.

Elephant-foot Drum Dance is the most popular dance for men in Xishuangbanna and has been listed in the National Protection Directory. The reason why it is called Elephant-foot Drum Dance is that when dancing, each dancer carries a drum shaped like an elephant's foot. The drums are made from hollowed mango trees or kapok trunks and covered with cowhide. The dance is characterized by strong rhythmic movements: hands beating the drum, feet tapping the ground, arching the chest and shrugging the shoulders. Elephant-foot Drum Dance is an indispensable activity on important festivals, therefore where there is the sound of elephant-foot drum, there are happy people.

Think and Discuss:

1. 根据一大学对学生的问卷调查，近一半的大学生不能坚持每天吃早饭，超四成学生有偏食挑食习惯，超三成学生"想吃什么就吃什么"，近八成学生饭后不运动，还有近四成学生因为饮食习惯曾患肠胃病。大学生应该如何养成良好的饮食习惯？

2. 我们应该节约和保护水资源，那么你觉得泼水节和节约用水是否矛盾呢？

3. 经济学家周天勇指出，几十层的高楼住宅，不符合人们的天性。一栋栋几十层的高楼，就是水泥、钢筋、玻璃和里边隔成小空间的大立柜，每家每户就像一个个鸽子间。未来的城市建设，应该保留低矮建筑、小巷小街和小桥流水。对此，你怎么看？钢筋水泥丛林到底都框住了些什么？

第三节　物华天宝　人杰地灵

西双版纳得天独厚的地理位置和气候条件，造就了其丰富的物产，在这片神奇富饶的土地上，同样英雄辈出，人才济济。

（一）热带水果

西双版纳堪称天然果园，得天独厚的地理位置培养了种类极其丰富的热带水果，因此常年水果不断。常见的有香蕉、菠萝、芒果、柚子、杨桃、菠萝蜜、荔枝、桂圆、椰子、蛋黄果、莲雾、火龙果、木瓜、山竹和西番莲等。

在西双版纳，人们尤其喜欢吃未成熟的青芒果，青芒果味道酸涩，直接吃往往难以下咽，所以需要调味。西双版纳气候湿热，人们喜欢吃酸辣，有利于排湿。芒果的酸，再配合其他的调料，可以创造出神奇的味觉体验。在西双版纳，用辣椒等香料调味的青芒果，可以算作一道菜。另外，菠萝蜜也是西双版纳颇具特色的一种水果，菠萝蜜又叫树菠萝，它是世界上最重的水果，可重达20公斤。它的果肉可以直接吃也可加工成罐头、果脯、果汁等，有止渴、补中益气的功效。种子富含淀粉，可煮后食用；菠萝蜜的树液和叶子还可药用，消肿解毒。上百年的菠萝蜜树，木色金黄，材质坚硬，可用来制作家具，还能做成黄色的染料。

（二）橡胶

橡胶是广泛用于国防建设、国民经济建设和人们生活的重要物资。西双版纳和海南岛是中国最大的两个天然橡胶基地。2021年，橡胶种植面积达447万亩，干胶产量达31.2万吨，已成为全国最大的橡胶种植和生产地。

（三）"橡胶大王"钱仿周

一直到 20 世纪中叶，中国还没有橡胶树的种植和天然橡胶的生产，只能从国外高价进口橡胶，还常常受到敌对国家的阻挠。不过有一个人却不服气，他觉得只要愿意精心培植，那么一定能够培育出适合中国种植的橡胶树。这个人就是爱国华侨钱仿周。抗日战争时期，他在东南亚经营橡胶园，赚了不少钱，但他从来没有忘记自己的祖国。当他了解到中国始终没有橡胶树时，便产生了为祖国引进橡胶树的想法。不过这并不容易，由于当时交通不便，路途又远，种子根本无法及时送回国内种植。钱仿周在泰国邀请华侨李宗周一起成立公司，共同经营橡胶事业。其间，由于局势动荡、人力单薄、自然灾害等原因，橡胶树种植试验困难重重。最终，钱仿周花了整整 10 年时间进行栽培，于 1955 年成功培育出了适合中国种植的橡胶树。

（四）普洱茶

西双版纳有着悠久的种茶历史，是名扬世界的普洱茶的原产地，也是世界上大叶种茶的发源地，最早关于西双版纳产茶的记载可以追溯到公元 8 世纪。明朝时期，西双版纳属普洱府管辖，加上西双版纳出产的茶叶都需经普洱府运往四面八方，普洱茶因此而得名。明朝后期，普洱茶被朝廷的官员看中，并送进京城，献给天子品尝，从此，普洱茶身价百倍。到了清朝，朝廷正式将普洱茶定为"贡茶"，西双版纳也由此变为"贡茶之乡"。中华人民共和国成立后，云南成立了茶叶研究机构并扩大了茶叶种植面积。

一般来说，普洱茶分生茶和熟茶。生茶是新鲜的茶叶采摘后以自然的方式陈放，未经过发酵处理的茶。生茶茶性较烈、刺激。新制或陈放不久的生茶有强烈的苦味、涩味，汤色较浅或黄绿，生茶对胃刺激较大，适合胃良好的人饮用。经过发酵等工艺加工而成的茶称为熟茶。熟茶色泽褐红，滋味纯和，具有独特的陈香。由于熟茶茶性温和，保健功能较好，很受大众喜爱。1984 年，现代普洱茶创始人吴启英通过科学技术方法，在保证普洱茶质量的情况下22天就完成了普洱熟茶的发酵转化。这是现代普洱熟茶的开端，为普洱熟茶批量生产并走向世界奠定了基础。

（五）小粒咖啡

除茶叶之外，咖啡历来也是西双版纳的重要商品。咖啡不仅含丰富的蛋白质、脂肪和蔗糖，还含有一定的淀粉和咖啡因等物质。经过烘焙加工制成饮料后，不仅香气浓郁，味道可口，而且营养丰富，还有很好的提神功效。因此，咖啡和茶叶、可可并称世界三大饮料，并位居榜首。云南咖啡属品质较好的阿拉比卡品种，一般称为云南小粒咖啡，已有一百多年的栽培历史。目前国内98%的咖啡产自云南，其产地主要分布在普洱、保山、德宏、临沧和西双版纳等地区。西双版纳出产的咖啡主要为小粒咖啡，其香气浓郁，风味独特，一部分在当地加工供应本土市场，另一部分主要出口，销往世界各地。

（六）小苞谷

由于得天独厚的自然地理环境，在西双版纳，一年四季都能吃到新鲜的玉米。自然种植的玉米，吸收了充足的阳光和水分，特别香甜软糯。当地有一种百年老品种，成熟的玉米只有成人的巴掌大小，当地人称"小苞谷"，这是非转基因和老品种的代名词，而外来的品种才被称为"玉米"。天然种植出来的小玉米，集色、香、味、黏于一身，淀粉、蛋白质、脂肪、维生素等营养元素含量远高于普通玉米。它比一般糯玉米要甜很多，又不像水果玉米那般纯甜。它的淀粉含量比普通玉米高10多倍，这也让它比一般的玉米更容易消化，很适合老人和小孩吃。

（七）樟脑与腰果

樟脑，是以樟树为原料提取的化工产品，主要用于医药和化工。天然樟脑在国际市场上很受欢迎，而我国只有福建、江西、云南和台湾等少数地区才产樟脑。西双版纳是云南的樟脑主要产地。在西双版纳，农民用传统方法提取出粗制的樟脑，工厂收购这些粗制樟脑并制作成樟脑精粉。樟脑也是西双版纳主要的出口商品之一，主要销往日本。

在西双版纳，还有一种有趣又可爱的植物，它的果实分为上、下两部分。上部由花托发育膨大而成，形状像一个梨，下部是一个月牙形状的坚硬小果实，因其形状像人的肾脏，因此被称为腰果。常见的腰果仁就是这一部分剥壳后的种仁，它与核桃、扁桃和榛子并列为世界著名的四大干果仁。腰果是热带重要的干果和油料树种，在我国腰果有 60 多年的种植历史，海南和西双版纳是其主要的种植地区。

（八）末代傣王——刀世勋

历史上，傣王又称召片领，是西双版纳傣族地区的最高统治者。刀世勋，1928 年 9 月出生，他曾是西双版纳的召片领，也就是西双版纳末代傣王。但自 1949 年起，他积极参加解放军组织的宣传队及工作队，并在此期间加入了共青团。后来他从云南大学历史系毕业，一生致力于民族语言文字工作。他不仅是中华人民共和国成立以来第一代大学生和研究生，还是国内外知名的民族语言学教授，编写了多部傣语汉语词典。他一生热爱社会主义，为云南边疆民族地区经济发展、民族团结、文化繁荣和社会稳定做出了积极贡献。

（九）孤胆英雄——岩龙

岩龙，战斗英雄，1960 年出生在西双版纳景洪，1978 年 3 月应征入伍加入中国人民解放军。入伍后的岩龙非常刻苦，一边学汉语，一边刻苦训练，练就了过硬的射击技术。1979 年参加对越自卫反击战。在战斗中，他曾孤身一人向敌人阵地隐蔽前进，到距越军不到百米处，突然射击，孤身奋战数小时，击毙越军二十余人。后来，在一次搜索残敌的战斗中，年仅

19岁的岩龙不幸中弹,光荣牺牲。为了表彰他英勇机智、孤胆战斗的英雄事迹,他被授予"孤胆英雄"称号。

(十)孔雀公主——刀美兰

刀美兰,1944年出生于西双版纳的景洪,是著名的舞蹈家。1954年,刀美兰被挑选进入西双版纳文工队,那时虽然条件简陋,训练却一点不含糊,小小的刀美兰坚持了下来。在改编自民间传说《召树屯》的舞蹈《召树屯与南吾诺娜》中,刀美兰扮演了"孔雀公主",从此结束了千百年来孔雀舞由男人扮跳的历史,她也成为中国舞台的第一个"孔雀公主"。这不仅开创了女子孔雀舞的先河,还对表演形式做了革新:去掉了面具,显出了"公主"美丽的真容。东方歌舞团成立后,刀美兰来到北京,并在大型音乐舞蹈史诗《东方红》中担任部分章节的领舞。刀美兰从未进入舞蹈学校进行过专业学习,自身的天赋、后天的勤奋以及滋养她的这片神奇的土地造就了她独特的舞蹈艺术魅力。

Section Three Natural Treasures and Outstanding People

The unique geographical location and climate conditions in Xishuangbanna create rich products and this magical and fertile land also nurtures many brave heroes and outstanding talents.

Tropical Fruits

Xishuangbanna can be called a natural orchard. Its unique geographical location helps to cultivate an extremely rich variety of tropical fruits, so there are many fruits all year round, such as banana, pineapple, mango, pomelo, carambola, jackfruit, litchi, longan, coconut, eggfruit, wax apple, pitaya, papaya, mangosteen, passion fruit and so on.

In Xishuangbanna, people especially like to eat unripe green mango. It tastes sour and astringent so that it is difficult to swallow directly without seasoning. Since the climate is hot and humid, people prefer sour and spicy flavors, which are conducive to moisture removal. The acidity of mango, combined with other spices, can create a magical taste. In Xishuangbanna, green mangoes seasoned with spices such as pepper can serve as a dish. Beside mango, jackfruit is also a special fruit in Xishuangbanna. As the heaviest fruit in the world, jackfruit is also called nangka and can reach the weight of 20 kilograms. Its flesh can either be eaten directly or processed into cans, preserves, juice and other products, which have the effect of quenching thirst and tonifying Qi. Its seeds are rich in starch and can be boiled and eaten. Jackfruit's sap and leaves can also be used for medicinal purposes, such as reducing swelling and detoxification. The wood of over one hundred-year-old jackfruit trees looks golden yellow and is extremely hard, which can be used to make furniture and yellow dyes.

Rubber

Rubber is an important material widely used in national defense, economic construction and people's daily lives. Xishuangbanna and Hainan are the two largest natural rubber bases in China. In 2021, the rubber planting area reached 4.47 million mu in Xishuangbanna, with a dry rubber output of 312 thousand tons, making it the largest rubber planting and processing area in China.

Qian Fangzhou, the "Rubber King"

There hadn't been any rubber trees planted or any natural rubber produced in China until the middle of 20th century. Rubber could only be imported at high prices from abroad, and it was often interfered with by hostile countries. However, one person was unwilling to accept it, believing that as long as he was determined to cultivate carefully, he would be able to find rubber trees suitable for China. This man was named Qian Fangzhou, a patriotic overseas Chinese. During the War of Resistance Against Japanese Aggression, he ran a rubber plantation in Southeast Asia and made a fortune, however, he never forgot his motherland. When he learned that there were no rubber trees in China, he came up with the idea of introducing rubber trees to China. However, it was not easy. Due to the inconvenient transportation and long distance, the seeds could not be sent back to China in time. Then, Qian Fangzhou asked Li Zongzhou to set up a company in Thailand to jointly manage the rubber business. During this period, the turbulent situation, the lack of workforce, and natural disasters all made it difficult to test the rubber trees. After 10 years' hard work, Qian Fangzhou successfully cultivated rubber trees suitable for China in 1955.

Pu'er Tea

Xishuangbanna has a long history of growing tea. It is not only the origin of the world-famous Pu'er tea, but also the birthplace of big-leaf tea in the world. The earliest records of tea production in Xishuangbanna can be traced back to the 8th century AD. During the Ming Dynasty, Xishuangbanna was under the administration of Pu'er, and the tea produced in Xishuangbanna had to be transported to other places from Pu'er, so it was named Pu'er tea. In the late Ming Dynasty, Pu'er tea was chosen by officials of the imperial court and sent to the capital to be tasted by the emperor. Since then, Pu'er tea had been famous and in the Qing Dynasty, the court officially designated it as "Royal Tea" (the tribute tea to imperial court), Xishuangbanna becoming the "hometown of the Royal Tea". After the founding of the People's Repubic of China, a tea research institute was established in Yunnan and the tea planting area was greatly expanded.

Generally speaking, Pu'er tea is divided into raw tea and cooked tea. Raw tea is aged in a natural way without being fermented and the taste is strong. The newly-made or shortly-aged raw tea has a strong bitter and astringent taste with a light or yellowish green color. Raw tea is more irritating to the stomach and is suitable for people without stomach diseases. Tea processed by fermentation and other techniques is called cooked tea. Cooked tea looks brown-red with a pure flavor and unique fragrance. Being quite mild and good for health, cooked tea is very popular among the public. In 1984, Wu Qiying, the founder of modern Pu'er tea, completed the fermentation of Pu'er cooked tea in 22 days under the condition of ensuring the quality by means of science and technology, which was the beginning of modern Pu'er cooked tea and laid the foundation for the mass production and exportation of cooked tea.

Yunnan Small-grain Coffee

Apart from tea, coffee has always been an important commodity in Xishuangbanna. Coffee is not only rich in protein, fat and sugar, but also contains substances like starch and caffeine. After baking and processing, coffee beans can be used to make beverages, which are not only rich in aroma, delicious in taste, but also nutritious and have a good refreshing effect. Therefore, coffee ranks first even if coffee, tea and cocoa are all regarded as the major drinks in the world. Yunnan coffee belongs to the Arabica variety known to have a better quality, and is called Yunnan small-grain coffee, with a planting history of more than a hundred years. Currently, 98% of the domestic coffee is produced in Yunnan, with the major producing areas in Pu'er,

Baoshan, Dehong, Lincang and Xishuangbanna. Coffee beans produced in Xishuangbanna are mainly small-grained with rich aroma and unique flavor. Some of them are processed locally and supplied to the local market, while the rest is mainly exported to all parts of the world.

Small Fresh Waxy Maize

In Xishuangbanna, fresh maize is available all the year round, due to the unique natural geographical environment. The naturally-grown maize is exposed to sufficient sunshine and water, making it especially sweet and soft. There is a century-old local variety, which is only the size of an adult's palm. It is known locally as "Small Bao Gu", a term synonymous with non-GM and old varieties, while the exotic variety is called "maize". Naturally-grown small maize, with a bright color, pleasant smell, sweet taste and sticky texture, is richer in starch, protein, fat, vitamin and other nutritional elements than ordinary maize. It is much sweeter than the usual waxy corn, but not as sweet as fruit corn. Its starch content is more than 10 times higher than that of ordinary corn, which also makes it easier to digest and therefore suitable for the elderly and children.

Camphor and Cashew Nuts

Camphor is a chemical product extracted from camphor trees, mainly used in medicine and chemical industry. Natural camphor is very popular in the international market, while in China, only a few areas such as Fujian, Jiangxi, Yunnan and Taiwan produce camphor. Xishuangbanna is the main producer of camphor in Yunnan. Farmers extract crude camphor through traditional methods, which is purchased by the factories and then made into camphor powder. Camphor is also one of the main export commodities of Xishuangbanna, mainly sold to Japan.

There is also an interesting and lovely plant in Xishuangbanna, with its fruit divided into the upper part and the lower part. The upper part is developed and expanded from the receptacle and was shaped like a pear; the lower part is a hard small fruit in the shape of a crescent. It is called "yaoguo" because it resembles a human kidney. The commonly seen cashew nut is the shelled kernel of this part and it is one of the four world-famous dry nuts together with walnut, almond and hazelnut. With a planting history of more than 60 years in China, cashew nut is an important dry fruit and oil tree species in the tropics, mainly planted in Hainan and Xishuangbanna.

The Last King of Dai—Dao Shixun

In history, the king of Dai, known as "Zhaopianling", was the supreme ruler of the Dai region in Xishuangbanna. Dao Shixun, born in September, 1928, he was "Zhaopianling" and became the last king of Dai. Since 1949, however, he had actively participated in the propaganda and working teams organized by the People's Liberation Army and also joined the Communist Youth League. Later, he graduated from the History Department of Yunnan University and dedicated his whole life to the work of national languages. Not only was he one of the first generation of college graduates and postgraduates in China, but he was also a well-known professor of national linguistics at home and abroad, who compiled many Dai-Chinese dictionaries. What's more, he had deep love for socialism for all his life and made great contributions to the economic development, national unity, cultural prosperity and social stability in Yunnan frontier ethnic areas.

The Lone Hero—Yan Long

Yan Long, a war hero, was born in Jinghong, Xishuangbanna, in 1960. He joined the People's Liberation Army in March, 1978 and worked very hard in the army.

In addition to taking rigorous training, he worked hard on his Chinese and acquired excellent shooting skills. He participated in the self-defense war against Vietnam in 1979. In a battle, he secretly advanced to the enemy position on his own, and when he was less than 100 meters away from the Vietnamese army, he began to shoot. Fighting alone for several hours, he killed more than 20 Vietnamese soldiers. Later, in a battle searching for the enemies, 19-year old Yan Long was shot to death and he was awarded the title of "Lone Hero" in recognition of his heroic deeds.

The Peacock Princess —Dao Meilan

Dao Meilan, born in 1944 in Jinghong, Xishuangbanna, is a famous dancer. In 1954, she was selected into the Art Team of Xishuangbanna. In spite of the poor conditions, the training was rigorous, however, little Meilan managed to withstand it. Later, in the dance *Zhao Shutun and Nanwu Nona* adapted from the folk legend *Zhao Shutun*, she played the role of "peacock princess", which ended the thousand-year history of peacock dance performed by men and she became the first "peacock princess" on the Chinese stage. It not only created the first female peacock dance, but also innovated the performance, showing the beautiful looks of the "princess" instead of wearing a mask. After the Oriental Song and Dance Troupe was founded, she went to Beijing and worked as the lead dancer in several chapters of the large-scale musical and dance epic *The East Is Red*. Although she had never had any professional training in a dance school, her own talent, diligence, together with the nourishment she got from this magical land, all contributed to her unique artistic charm of dance art.

Think and Discuss:

1. 一骑红尘妃子笑，无人知是荔枝来。在古代，热带水果仅限于宫廷，而现在，全国各地大大小小的超市均有供应，这种变化的原因是什么？这种变化可能带来的消极影响是什么？

2. 有人呼吁，国家和地方主流媒体应该适当减少纯娱乐节目的比重和时间，减少青少年对流量明星的追捧，同时增加对重大科技事件和优秀科技人员事迹的宣传报道，进而弘扬科学家精神。你同意这种观点吗？

3. 咖啡和茶都是世界三大饮品之一，它们都含咖啡因，能让我们持续地保持活力，但渐渐地，咖啡受到年轻人的追捧，茶似乎成了中年人才会喝的饮品。你更喜欢茶还是咖啡？从茶和咖啡中能看出中西方文化的哪些不同？

第四节　树木丛生　百草丰茂

西双版纳是中国热带生态系统保存最完整的地区，全州有森林面积约155万公顷，有2个国家级保护区，占地约400万亩，其中70万亩为保护完好的原始森林。西双版纳有高等植物5 000多种，其中特有植物达153种，如望天树等，濒危植物也有134种。众多的植物种属相互交错生长，形成了复杂多样的植被景观。另外，全州还有中草药1 700多种，经过鉴定的就达到500多种。

（一）榕树

在西双版纳，生长着很多榕树。榕树是个"大家庭"，有几十个不同的品种。榕树最高可达30米，其枝干可向四面无限伸展。支柱根和枝干交织在一起，看上去像稠密的丛林，因此被称为"独木成林"。在热带雨林里，具有绞杀功能的榕树有二三十种。它们往往选择一些高大挺拔的寄主作为绞杀对象，从而获得更广阔的生态位，寄主在被绞杀死亡之后，还能为之提供更多的营养物质。绞杀现象是植物之间的一种很残酷的现象，类似于动物界的弱肉强食。

榕树的果实坚硬，不易消化，当它的果实被动物食用后，种子会随着它们的粪便随处洒落。榕树的生命力极强，当种子撒在空旷的地面时，榕树可以直挺挺地单独生长。当榕树的种子落在一些高大挺拔的大树上，或者当它紧挨着其他大树生长时，它的主干就会像蟒蛇一样紧紧地缠绕着大树生长。种子一旦发芽存活，很快就能长出纵横交错、杀气腾腾的气生根系，它们会逐渐包裹寄主的树干并上下蔓延。深入土地的根与茂盛的枝叶相连，形成"独木成林"和"树瀑"的奇观。被绞杀的寄主植物逐渐会因外部绞杀和内部养分的贫乏而枯萎、死亡。榕树这个"杀手"最终会成为一株独立茂盛的大树。

（二）望天树

传说在很久很久以前，天上的神仙总是喜欢往地上撒一些花，这就是人们常说的"天女散花"。这些被撒下的花的种子经过多年漫长的努力，根据各自的目标，演变成世界上不同的植物。有的成为象征爱情的玫瑰，有的成了以掠夺的方式壮大自己的绞杀榕。还有一种植物，总希望看一看故乡的样子，于是，它不停地长啊长，最后长到了令人羡慕的高度，成了最靠近天堂的植物。它就是被称为"雨林的巨人"的望天树。望天树是西双版纳州特有的树种之一，是国家级保护珍稀植物。它高大挺拔，高度可达七八十米，是我国长得最高的阔叶树种，有"林中巨人""林中美王子"的美誉。

20世纪60年代以前，由于交通闭塞等方面的因素，西双版纳勐腊的望天树这一珍稀热带雨林植物一直无人知晓，国外热带雨林专家通过地理位置分析就片面地否定了中国热带雨林的存在。直到70年代中期，我国著名植物学家蔡希陶教授亲自到勐腊进行实地考察并取样鉴定，终于发现了热带雨林树种望天树，以此充分证实了我国热带雨林的存在，中国成为世界上森林类型最完整的国家之一。位于勐腊县的西双版纳望天树景区是中国唯一被世界公认的热带雨林。

望天树景区的标志性景点是一棵高达60米的望天树，它的存在证实了我国存在热带雨林，有很大的意义。景区里还有两条小路也很有名且意义非凡，它们分别是菲利普小道和蔡希陶小道。菲利普小道是为了纪念当时的世界爱护野生动物基金会主席爱丁堡公爵菲利普亲王，是他亲自到西双版纳考证，确认了望天树的存在，并且向世界宣布中国西双版纳热带雨林的存在。蔡希陶小道则是纪念望天树的发现者——我国著名的植物学家蔡希陶。

（三）王莲

王莲原产于南美洲亚马孙河流域，是一种典型的热带植物，只有在热带地区的夏季才能欣赏到它独具魅力的身姿。王莲具有世界上水生植物中最大的叶片，叶的边缘向上卷曲，就像一只只浮在水面上的翠绿色大玉盘。王莲巨大的叶片，正面呈现淡淡的绿色，十分光滑，背面呈土红色，密布着中空而坚实的粗壮叶脉，构成坚固的"骨架"，叶子里面有许多充满气体的洼窝，这使叶子具有很大的浮力，最多可承重六七十千克。2021年7月，西双版纳热带植物园内的王莲叶片直径达到了1.92米，是六十年来历史上的最大直径，并有望通过后期的管理养护突破两米大关。

（四）跳舞草

人会跳舞不稀奇，动物会跳舞也不稀奇，你能想象植物也会跳舞吗？在西双版纳，就生长着一种会跳舞的植物——跳舞草。跳舞草是一种具有"灵性"的植物，只要听到优美的音乐，或者有人对着它唱歌，它的叶片就会随着音乐的节奏开始舞动。跳舞草为什么会跳舞呢？人们一直在探索其中的奥秘。据目前的研究发现，跳舞草叶片的叶柄处的细胞里有一种海绵体，这种海绵体对中低频率，即35~65分贝的声音有共振作用。跳舞草不只会跳舞，还具有药用保健价值，全株可供药用，有舒筋活络、祛痰化瘀的功效。

Section Four　Luxuriant Plants

Xishuangbanna is the region with the most complete preservation of tropical ecosystem in China. There are about 1.55 million hectares of forests, and 2 national nature reserves which cover an area of about 4 million mu, of which well-protected virgin forests occupy about 0.7 million mu. There are more than 5,000 kinds of higher plants, including 153 species of endemic plants, such as the sky tree, and 134 species of endangered plants. Plants of different species interlace with one another, forming a complex and diverse vegetation landscape. In addition, there are more than 1,700 kinds of Chinese herbal medicines, among which more than 500 have been authenticated.

Banyan Tree

There are many banyan trees in Xishuangbanna. Banyan is a "big family" with dozens of different varieties. It can reach up to 30 meters high, and its branches can stretch infinitely in all directions. The pillar roots and branches are intertwined, which looks like a dense jungle, so it is called "a single tree into a forest". In the tropical rain forest, there are twenty or thirty kinds of banyan trees capable of strangulation. They often target the tall and straight host trees to obtain a broader ecological niche and the host can provide even more nutrients after being killed. Strangulation is a very cruel phenomenon among plants, which is similar to the law of the jungle among animals.

The fruit of banyan is hard and difficult to digest. When it is eaten by animals, the seeds will be scattered everywhere with their feces. With strong vitality, banyan can grow straight and alone even if the seeds fall on the open ground. When a banyan grows next to other trees or when the seeds fall on other tall and straight trees, its trunk will grow tightly around the tree like a python. Once the seeds germinate, they will soon develop crisscross and murderous aerial roots, which will gradually wrap the trunk of the host and spread up and down. Then the roots, deeply connected with the vigorous branches and thick leaves, form the spectacles of "a single tree into a forest" and "tree waterfall". Gradually, the strangled host trees eventually wither and die due to the external strangulation and the lack of internal nutrients, while banyan, the "killer", will eventually become an independent and flourishing tree.

The Sky Tree

Legend has it that a long time ago, the gods in the heaven liked to sprinkle flowers on the ground, which was called "The heavenly maids scatter blossoms". After years of efforts, the seeds of these flowers evolved into different plants according to their respective goals. For example, some became roses symbolizing love, and some developed into banyan trees surviving in a predatory way. There was also a plant who always wanted to take a look at its hometown, so it kept growing. Finally, it grew to an amazing height and became the plant closest to heaven. It is called sky tree (parashorea chinensis), which is regarded as "the giant in the rainforest". Sky tree is one of the unique tree species in Xishuangbanna and is a rare plant protected at the national level. Being both tall and straight, with its height up to 70 or 80 meters, it is the highest broad-leaved tree species in China and enjoys the reputation of "giant in the forest" and "prince of the forest".

Before the 1960s, due to traffic blockage and other factors, sky tree, the rare tropical rain forest plant in Mengla, Xishuangbanna was unknown. Foreign tropical rain forest experts unilaterally denied the existence of tropical rain forest in China based on the analysis of geographical location. In the mid-1970s, professor Cai Xitao, a famous botanist in China, personally went to Mengla for a field investigation. After sampling and identification, he finally found the tree species of tropical rain forests—sky tree, which fully confirmed the existence of tropical rain forest in China. Since then, China has been recognized as one of the countries with the most complete forest types in the world. The Sky Tree Scenic Spot located in Mengla County is the only tropical rain forest of China recognized by the world.

The iconic view spot of Sky Tree Scenic Spot is a 60-meter-high sky tree. It is this tree that confirms the existence of tropical rain forest in China, so it is of great significance. There are also two famous paths in the area: Philip Trail and Cai Xitao Trail. Philip Trail is to commemorate the president of the World Wildlife Fund of that time, Prince Philip, the Duke of Edinburgh. It was he who went to Xishuangbanna in person to verify and confirm and finally announced the existence of tropical rain forest to the world. Cai Xitao Trail commemorates the discoverer of sky tree—Cai Xitao, the famous botanist in China.

Victoria Amazonica

Victoria Amazonica is native to the Amazon River Basin in South America. Since it is a typical tropical plant, its unique charm can be appreciated only in the summer of the tropics. It has the largest leaf among aquatic plants in the world. The edge of the leaf curls upward, just like a large emerald jade plate floating on the water. The front of the huge leaves is light green and very smooth, while the back is earthy red and densely covered with hollow and solid thick leaf veins forming a solid "skeleton". There are many air-filled pits in the leaves, making the leaves have great buoyancy and bear up to 60 or 70 kilograms. In July 2021, the diameter of the Victoria Amazonica's leaves in the Tropical Botanical Garden reached 192 centimeters, which is the largest in the history of 60 years, and is expected to reach beyond two meters through careful maintenance.

Dancing Plant

It is not uncommon for people and animals to dance. Can you imagine plants can dance? In Xishuangbanna, there is a plant which can dance and is regarded as a "spiritual" plant. As long as it hears beautiful music or someone singing to it, its leaves will begin to dance. Why does the plant dance? People have been exploring the mystery. According to the current research, there is a kind of sponge in the cells at the petiole of the leaflet, which resonates with the sound of low and medium frequency (35—65 decibels). Dancing plant not only dances, but also has medicinal and health care values. The whole plant can be used for medicine with the effects of relaxing muscles, activating collaterals and removing phlegm and blood stasis.

Think and Discuss:

1. 人生道路并非一帆风顺，苦难和坎坷随时会袭来。对于看似弱小的对手或缺点，如果不能保持警惕，长此以往，它可能会发展到无法控制。因此，刘备告诫儿子勿以恶小而为之；欧阳修提醒人们祸患常积于忽微，智勇多困于所溺。从榕树的绞杀现象中，你还能得到哪些启示？

2. 《生物多样性公约》第十五次缔约方大会在云南昆明举办，这与云南丰富的生物多样性密不可分。云南生态系统复杂多样，有各类珍稀动物、植物和微生物，人类与自然和谐共存，使得云南成为全球著名的"植物王国""动物王国"和"世界花园"。你认为保护生物多样性有哪些意义？

第五节　孔雀南飞此处栖，象群河谷自由行

西双版纳有野生动物756种，占全国的25.3%。其中，已知哺乳动物108种，鸟类427种，爬行野生动物70多种，被列为国家重点保护的珍稀动物有多达109种。在西双版纳还保存着中国最大的野生亚洲象种群，还较为集中地分布着野牛、印支虎、绿孔雀、巨蜥、蟒等珍稀动物。

（一）野生亚洲象

据考古发现证明，亚洲象曾广泛地分布在长江流域、两广及贵州地区，甚至北至黄河流域。随着气候和地理环境的变化，亚洲象被迫一路南迁。由于屡遭猎杀和破坏，野生的亚洲象数量十分稀少。现在，野生亚洲象属于国家一级保护动物，西双版纳是它们在中国唯一的栖息地。

2021年5月，原生活在西双版纳国家级自然保护区的十几头亚洲象突然开始北迁，造访玉溪及红河，并受到社会广泛关注。据调查显示，不少野象更喜欢在保护区外游荡，而非生活在保护区。由于保护力度不断加大，西双版纳国家级自然保护区森林覆盖率逐年增加，导致亚洲象主要食物野芭蕉等植物逐步变为不可食用的木本植物。亚洲象的食物日益减少，使得象群逐步活动到保护区外觅食。

值得庆幸的是，此次北迁亚洲象群尚未造成人员伤亡。这跟近年来云南省持续推进野生亚洲象监测和保护直接相关。未来将采取更多的措施防止象群北迁，引导其逐步返回普洱或西双版纳的栖息地，有效保护亚洲象群。

《最后一头战象》

动物小说大王沈石溪的小说《最后一头战象》讲述了一头西双版纳大

象的故事。在抗日战争时，一头名叫嘎羧的战象最后幸存了下来，但它知道自己大限将至，便再次披上它的象鞍，独自来到打洛江畔缅怀战友和往事，凭吊战场，最后它在埋葬着战友的"百象冢"旁刨开一个坑，庄严地把自己掩埋在了里面。

（二）孔雀

孔雀被视为"百鸟之王"，是最美丽的观赏鸟，也是吉祥、善良、美丽、华贵的象征。雄孔雀开屏的时候，会不停地做出各种各样优美的舞蹈动作，向雌孔雀炫耀自己的美丽，以此吸引雌孔雀。待到它求偶成功之后，便与雌孔雀一起产卵育雏。傣族人喜爱孔雀，因为他们认为孔雀能够给人带来吉祥。

"孔雀公主"的传说

"孔雀公主"是西双版纳地区广泛流传的傣族民间传说。相传在几百年前的西双版纳，一位部落头领的儿子长得英俊潇洒、聪明强悍。一天，他忠实的猎人朋友对他说："明天，有七位美丽的姑娘会飞到郎丝娜湖来游泳，其中最聪明美丽的是最小的七公主，你藏起她的孔雀衣，她就会留下来做你的妻子。"第二天，果然从远方飞来了七只孔雀，落到湖边就变成了七位年轻的姑娘。她们跳舞、游泳和戏水，尤其是最小的那位姑娘，漂亮极了！后来，头领的儿子藏起了她的孔雀衣，等她的姐姐们都飞走了，才捧着孔雀衣走了出来。两人一见钟情，头领的儿子娶到了自己心爱的姑娘。但是成婚不久，战争就爆发了，为了保卫自己的家园，他带兵出征，却节节败退，家园快要失守。有个恶毒的巫师借此向他父亲进谗言，要杀七公主。当七公主站在刑场上时，她泪流满面，跳起孔雀舞，身影消失在了空中。

Section Five Peacocks Flying South and Perching Here, Elephants Traveling Freely in the Valley

There are 756 species of wild animals in Xishuangbanna, accounting for 25.3% in China. Among them, there are 108 kinds of known mamals, 427 kinds of birds, over 70 species of reptile wild animals. As many as 109 species of rare animals are listed as key national protection. The largest wild Asian elephant group is also preserved in Xishuangbanna and other rare animals such as bison, Indo-Chinese tiger, green peacock, giant lizard and python also gather here.

Wild Asian Elephants

According to archaeological discoveries, Asian elephants were widely distributed in the Yangtze River Basin, Guangdong, Guangxi, Guizhou, and even north to the Yellow River Basin. With the change of the climate and geographical environment, Asian elephants constantly migrated southward. Because of serious poaching, hunting and other damages, the population of Asian elephants plunged to new low. Now, wild Asian elephants are listed as national first-class protected animals, and Xishuangbanna is the only habitat for them in China.

In May 2021, more than a dozen Asian elephants originally living in Xishuangbanna National Nature Reserve suddenly began to move north to Yuxi and Honghe, which attracted extensive attention from the society. According to the survey, many wild elephants prefer to wander outside rather than live in the reserve. Due to the increasing protection, the forest coverage of Xishuangbanna National Nature Reserve has increased year by year, resulting in the gradual evolution of plants such as wild plantain, the main food of Asian elephants, into inedible woody plants. The edible plants of Asian elephants keep decreasing, forcing the elephant groups to gradually move outside the reserve to look for food.

Fortunately, the northward migration of Asian elephants has not caused casualties. This is directly related to the continuous promotion of wild Asian elephant monitoring and protection in Yunnan Province in recent years. In the future, more measures will be taken to prevent elephant herds from moving north, and guide them to gradually return to the habitat of Pu'er or Xishuangbanna, and effectively protect the elephants.

The Last War Elephant

The Last War Elephant, an animal novel by the famous animal novelist Shen Shixi, tells a story about an elephant in Xishuangbanna. During the War of Resistance Against Japanese Aggression, an elephant named Gasuo finally survived. Knowing that he was doomed to death, he put on his elephant saddle again and came alone to the bank of Daluo River to visit the battlefield, mourning for his battle companions and cherishing the memory of the past. In the end, he dug a pit next to the tomb of his comrades and solemnly buried himself in it.

Peacock

Regarded as the "king of birds", peacock is not only the most beautiful ornamental bird, but also a symbol of auspiciousness, kindness, beauty and nobility. When the male peacock displays his feathers, he will keep making all kinds of beautiful dance movements, showing off his beauty to the female to attract her. After the successful courtship, they will hatch eggs and cultivate the young together. Dai people like peacocks, believing they can bring good luck.

The Legend of "Peacock Princess"

"Peacock Princess" is a Dai folklore widely spread in Xishuangbanna. Hundreds of years ago in Xishuangbanna, the son of a tribal chief was handsome, smart and strong. One day, his loyal hunter friend said to him, "Seven beautiful girls will fly to Langsina Lake to swim tomorrow. Among them, the youngest one, the seventh princess, is the smartest and most beautiful one. If you hide her peacock coat, she would stay and be your wife." The next day, seven peacocks flew from a distance, and as soon as they landed at the lakeside, they became seven young girls. They were dancing, swimming and splashing water. How beautiful was the youngest girl! The son of the chief hid her peacock coat and didn't show up with it in his hands until her sisters flew away. The two fell in love at the first sight and the man got married to his beloved girl. Soon after the marriage, the war broke out. In order to protect his homeland, the young man led troops to fight against the enemy. However, he was defeated and kept retreating, and his homeland was about to fall. A vicious wizard took this opportunity to slander his father to kill the seventh princess. When she stood on the execution ground, she burst into tears, performed the peacock dance, and then disappeared into the air.

Think and Discuss:

有人认为圈养大象是比野外保护更好的方式，因为大象表演可以让更多人喜欢并保护大象。但也有研究表明，大象具有较强的自我意识，有复杂的社群需求，并不适合人工圈养，大象表演及其背后的训练更是对动物身心的摧残。对此，你怎么看？

第六节　巧夺天工　匠心独具

贝叶经制作技艺不仅是云南西双版纳地方传统技艺，也是国家级非物质文化遗产之一。贝叶经是指刻写在经过处理的贝叶棕上的佛经，是用民间制作的铁笔将文字刻写在贝叶棕树叶之上制作而成。贝叶棕是一种热带植物，经过多道传统特殊工艺处理后，能防虫、防水、防变形，用它抄写的经书，能够历经千百年保存下来。

傣锦，即西双版纳傣族的织锦，是流传在民间的一种古老的手工纺织工艺品，具有浓郁的地方特色。傣锦织工精巧，图案别致，色彩艳丽，既漂亮又耐用。

慢轮制陶技艺是一项拥有四千多年历史的原始传统手工制陶术，在西双版纳至今被完整保留下来。制陶工具一般由大小花纹不同的木陶拍、卵石、竹片、小簸箕等组成，原料是当地盛产的黏土。工艺特点为慢轮手工制作，器物表面均用有刻纹的木拍拍打印纹，与南方出土的新石器时期的印纹陶器非常相似，这也证明慢轮制陶完整保存了远古时期的制陶技术。

Section Six　Superb Workmanship and Unique Ingenuity

The skills of making pattra-leaf scripture is not only the local traditional craftsmanship in Xishuangbanna, but also one of the national intangible cultural heritages. Pattra-leaf scripture refers to the Buddhist sutra engraved on the processed pattra; the script is engraved on the leaves with a civilian-made iron pen. Pattra is a tropical plant and its leaves can prevent insects, water and deformation after many traditional and special processes, therefore, the scriptures on pattra leaves can be preserved for thousands of years.

Dai brocade is an ancient hand-made textile handicraft popular among Dai people in Xishuangbanna, with a strong local characteristic. Because of the exquisite weaving skills, unique patterns and gorgeous colors, Dai brocade is both beautiful and durable.

Slow-wheel pottery making skill is a primitive traditional pottery making technique with a history of more than 4,000 years, which has been completely preserved in Xishuangbanna. The major tools include different sizes and patterns of wooden bats, pebbles, bamboo scrapers, and small dustpans and so on. The raw material is mainly the locally-abundant clay. The most distinctive feature is the procedure of slow-wheel manual manufacturing during which decorative patterns on pottery surfaces are made by using a wooden bat. The patterns are similar to those of stamped pottery unearthed from the Neolithic site in south China, which is a proof that it completely preserves the pottery making skills in ancient times.

Think and Discuss:

人们对"纯手工"有种特殊情愫,相较于流水线上千篇一律的产品,人们更倾向于"做工粗劣"、带着天然质感的产品,因为它们每一件都是独一无二的。然而,快节奏的生活,巨大的市场需求,让传统手工制作显得无比滞后,越来越多的传统手工艺慢慢流失。对于这些手工艺的传承和保护,你有什么好的建议呢?

第七节 相知无远近 万里尚为邻

西双版纳中缅、中老边境的人们,千百年来互相通婚、通商,关系密切,往来频繁。西双版纳与邻近的泰国、缅甸和老挝在历史、文化、生活习俗等方面有很多相同的地方,因此,在边境上,人们自古以来就保持着密切的贸易往来和交流。目前,西双版纳有4个公路、水运、航空国家级口岸,具有对外开放的巨大潜力和优势。从西双版纳嘎洒国际机场可以直飞老挝琅勃拉邦、泰国清迈和清莱,还有柬埔寨暹粒等城市。景洪市的客运站也有开往琅勃拉邦和缅甸小勐拉等境外城市的国际班车。从西双版纳的关累港也可坐船到泰国清盛港。我国与老挝合力建造的中老国际铁路也已通车,从西双版纳向北3个小时可达省会昆明,向南2个小时可到老挝琅勃拉邦省,4个小时可到老挝首都万象。西双版纳是云南省16个州市中唯一能通过水、陆、空立体交通直达老挝、缅甸、泰国三国的"南大门",是云南省对外交流的重要窗口。

Section Seven   Though Bosom Friends Miles Apart, No Distance If Sharing a Heart

People living on the China-Laos and China-Myanmar border in Xishuangbanna have been intermarrying and trading with one another for thousands of years, and keeping close relations and frequent exchanges. People in Xishuangbanna share many similarities with people in the neighboring Thailand, Myanmar and Laos in history, culture, living customs and so on.

Therefore, the inhabitants of the border areas have been maintaining close trade and exchanges since ancient times. At present, there are 4 national ports of highway, water transportation and aviation in Xishuangbanna, so it has great potential and advantages in opening up to the outside world. There are non-stop flights to Luang Prabang, Chiang Mai, Chiang Choi, Siem Reap, and other cities from Gasa International Airport. In the passenger station in Jinghong City, there are also international shuttle buses to Luang Prabang, Mongla and other overseas cities. From Guanlei Port, ships to Chiang Saen of Thailand are also available. The China-Laos Railway jointly built by China and Laos has been opened to traffic. From Xishuangbanna, it takes 3 hours to reach Kunming, the provincial capital of Yunnan, 2 hours to Luang Prabang Province in Laos, and 4 hours to Vientiane, the capital of Laos. As an important window for foreign exchanges, Xishuangbanna is the only "South Gate" among the 16 prefectures and cities in Yunnan Province that leads directly to Laos, Myanmar and Thailand through water, land and air transportation.

> **Think and Discuss:**
> 2021年底，中老铁路建成通车，这条铁路的开通有什么积极的影响和意义？

第五章 香格里拉篇
Chapter V Shangri-La

第一节 人间胜景 香格里拉

香格里拉位于云南省西北部滇、藏、川三省区交界处，是云南省海拔最高的地方。这里群山集结，江河深切，草原辽阔，森林茂密，共同组成了香格里拉多姿多彩的诱人景色。香格里拉市为中心的迪庆州境内，怒江、澜沧江、金沙江三江并流，呼啸南下，由西向东形成怒山山脉、澜沧江、云岭山脉、金沙江、中甸雪山山脉相间排列的三岭两江的格局，是世界一流的地质、地貌自然遗迹区。

（一）壮美的雪山冰川

迪庆境内沿怒山山脉的梅里雪山、太子雪山、碧罗雪山和云岭山脉、中甸大雪山岭脊分布有近千座雪山，迪庆堪称雪山林立之区。梅里雪山在德钦县境内，是康巴地区最著名的神山之一。山峰雪峰林立，主峰卡瓦格博为云南最高峰。其两侧并排错落的群峰之下，有冰库、冰川，向下延伸于山谷之中。春暖时节，冰水破冰而出，汹涌奔流，成为众多山泉的源头。

迪庆分布着广泛的碳酸盐类岩石，在冰川溶洞、溶蚀等作用下，形成了很多独特的高山喀斯特地貌。白水台是中国最大的泉华台地之一，位于香格里拉市白地村海拔 2580 米的山坡上。远眺白水台，似一块镶嵌在白地村上方的巨型白玉；近看白水台，宛若一个盛满琼浆玉露的大玉盘层层叠叠，耀眼夺目。

（二）雄伟的大江峡谷

迪庆州境内，由于横断山脉南北向的断裂，金沙江、澜沧江两条大江，沿着纵谷呼啸奔腾南下。怒山、云岭、贡嘎山脉夹着两江，形成两条巨大的峡谷，谷岭相差4000米。

金沙江古称"神川""丽水""泸水"。相传以盛产金沙而得名，是我国的第一大江——长江的上游。由四川流入迪庆境内，把高山切割成十分壮丽的险境，两岸危崖耸立，冰峰峥嵘，弯弯曲曲，江水被两岸的红石山岩紧紧地挤压，激流搏击，声响撼谷。到虎跳峡口附近的200千米以内，江面开阔，澎湃的怒涛变为平静的江流，可见木船往返。在石鼓附近，金沙江忽然急转向北，形成"长江第一湾"。再往下35千米处，宽阔平缓的江面渐渐变窄，江水似千军万马，向着一个深切的峡谷汹涌而进，便是哈巴雪山和玉龙雪山之间世界著名的大峡谷——虎跳峡。虎跳峡全长23千米，险滩18处，其落差达213米，江面最窄处20多米。从谷底到山峰，海拔相对高差3900米。虎跳峡最为壮观的时节是雨季江水上涨期：站立谷底，抬头仰望，两边群峰直通天际，悬崖峭壁直劈江中；望江心，飞流汹涌，惊涛拍岸，如万马奔腾，似电闪雷鸣。惊、险、奇、绝在这里表现得淋漓尽致。江心有一虎跳石，高达13米，如同阻止两山重合的中流砥柱。金沙江是三江并流中的大哥，而虎跳峡则是大哥身上的一颗明珠。其汹涌澎湃之势不只是让你叹为观止，而是实实在在的心灵上的震撼。

（三）立体分布的气候

迪庆属于温带和寒温带季风气候，但具有明显的低纬度高原季风气候特征，太阳辐射强，紫外线强。迪庆高原的气候既具备南亚次大陆广大地区干湿季分明的气候特征，又兼有内陆性气候特点。长达半年的冬季里，迪庆地区空气变得干燥，晴日多，气温低。剩下的半年，来自印度洋、孟加拉湾热带海洋的西南季风和来自南海的东南季风挟带着大量水汽涌向云贵高原。受到各山脉的阻挡,强度大为减弱,但还是较为湿润和温暖。由于其地势垂直性的变化,热量和水分随海拔的升高也出现垂直性的变化,于是出现人们所说的"一山分四季,隔里不同天"。一山浓缩了整个北半球的气候类型。

如此强烈的地势起伏和显著的环境条件差异造就了多样的植被分布,森林覆盖率高,是名副其实的高原醉氧吧。同时,迪庆拥有云南省最大的天然牧场和丰富的草场资源、动植物资源,是我国弥足珍贵的物种基因库。

Section One Shangri-La—the Fairyland on Earth

Shangri-La is located in the northwest of Yunnan Province, at the junction of Yunnan, Tibet and Sichuan. It is the highest-altitude county in Yunnan Province. The gathered mountains, deep rivers, vast grasslands and dense forests constitute the colorful and attractive scenery of Shangri-La. In Diqing Tibetan Autonomous Prefecture, with Shangri-La as the center, the Nujiang River, Lancang River and Jinsha River flow side by side. From west to east, the three rivers roar through Nushan mountains, Yunling mountains, and Zhongdian Snow mountains, which form a pattern of three mountains and two rivers. It is a geological and geomorphological natural relic area in the world.

Magnificent Snow-Capped Glaciers

There are nearly 1,000 magnificent snow-capped mountains along the Nushan mountains, including Meili Snow Mountain, Taizi Snow Mountain, Biluo Snow Mountain, Yunling mountain and Zhongdian Snow Mountains in Diqing. Diqing can be called an area full of snow mountains. Meili Snow

Mountain, located in Deqing County, is one of the most famous sacred mountains in Kangba area. There are many snow peaks, and Kawakarp, the main peak, is the highest peak in Yunnan. Under the scattered peaks on both sides, there are ice banks and glaciers extending downward into the valley. In the warm spring season, the ice water breaks through the ice and flows violently, becoming the source of many mountain springs.

A wide range of carbonate rocks are distributed in Diqing. Under the action of glaciers caves and dissolution, many unique alpine karst landforms have been formed. Baishuitai is one of the largest tufa platforms in China. It is located on the hillside which is 2,380 meters above sea level in Baidi village, Shangri-La City. Overlooked, it looks like a huge white jade inlaid above Baidi village; but when you look closely, it looks like a large dazzling jade plate full of good wine.

Majestic Rivers and Valleys

In Diqing Tibetan Autonomous Prefecture, due to the north-south deep faults of the Hengduan Mountains, the Jinsha River and Lancang River roar south along the longitudinal valley. The two rivers are sandwiched by Nushan mountains, Yunling mountains and Gongga mountains. Then two huge canyons, with a difference of 4,000 meters, have been formed.

Jinsha River was called "Shenchuan", "Lishui" or "Lushui" in ancient times. It is said that it's named after the abundance of sand. It is the upper reaches of the Yangtze River, the largest river in China. The river flows from Sichuan to Diqing, and the mountains are cut into a magnificent dangerous place. The cliffs on both sides are towering, and the ice peaks are winding. The river water is tightly squeezed by the red rocks on both sides, the flow crash on shores and the sound shakes the valley. Within 200 kilometers near the mouth of Tiger Leaping Gorge, the river is wide open, and the surging waves turn into a calm river flow. Wooden boats can be seen going back and forth. Near Shigu, the Jinsha River suddenly turns to the north, forming the "First Bend of the Yangtze River". Another 35 kilometers down, the wide and gentle river gradually narrows, and then surges towards a deep canyon, which is the world-famous grand canyon between Haba Snow mountain and Yulong Snow Mountain—Tiger Leaping Gorge. It has a total length of 23 kilometers, 18 thrilling shoals, with a drop about 213 meters, and the narrowest part of the river is about 20 meters. From the bottom of the valley to the peak, the relative altitude difference is nearly 3,900 meters. The most spectacular view of Tiger Leaping Gorge is during the rising period of river water in rainy season. When you stand at the bottom of the valley and look up, you can see the peaks on both sides lead to the sky, and the cliffs cut into the river. While you look down the river, you will see the turbulent current, and the surging waves beat the shore. It sounds like ten thousand horses crashing, as well as the lightning and thunder, which evokes the feeling of thrill, danger, quaintness and uniqueness. There is a Tiger Leaping Stone in the middle of the river, up to 13 meters high, which is like the mainstay to prevent the overlapping of the two mountains. If Jinsha River is the eldest brother in the three paralleled rivers, Tiger Leaping Gorge is a pearl on the eldest brother. Its surging momentum is not just breathtaking, but a real shock to the heart.

The Three-Dimensional Distributed Climate

Diqing belongs to monsoon climate in temperate and cold temperate zone, but with obvious characteristics of low latitude plateau monsoon climate, strong solar radiation and ultraviolet. The climate of Diqing plateau not only has distinct dry and wet seasons in the vast area of the South Asian subcontinent, but also has the feature of inland climate. During the long half-year winter, the air in Diqing becomes dry, with many sunny days but low temperatures. In the remaining six months, the southwest monsoon from the Indian Ocean, the tropical ocean of the Bay of Bengal and the southeast monsoon from the South China Sea rush to the Yunnan-Guizhou Plateau with a large amount of water vapor. Blocked by the mountains, its intensity is greatly weakened, but it is still wet and warm. Due to the vertical change of terrain, the heat and moisture conditions change with the altitude. So a saying goes that a mountain is divided into four seasons, and there are different days in the next place. The climate types of the whole northern hemisphere are condensed in a mountain.

Such strong topographic relief and significant differences in environmental conditions have created a variety of vegetation distribution and high forest coverage. It is a veritable plateau oxygen bar. At the same time, Diqing has the largest natural pasture, and rich grassland, animal and plant resources in Yunnan Province. It is a precious species gene bank in China.

Think and Discuss

香格里拉独特的自然地理条件造就了惊世绝俗的自然景观和生态的多样性，雨崩村就因其全国唯一"遗世独立"的地方的称号而名声大噪，但随着公路、电力、网络的修通，以及旅游行业的迅猛发展，当地的生态系统也受到了一定的影响，那应当如何平衡经济发展和生态环境的关系呢？

第二节　高原的馈赠　享美食之旅

特殊的自然地理和历史文化，使得香格里拉拥有众多的地方特产，如青稞、冬虫夏草、松茸、红景天、雪莲花等自然特产，又如青稞酒、酥油茶、牦牛肉等特产。

（一）青稞

青稞是当地人最主要的粮食作物，栽培历史悠久，种植面积广。青稞籽营养丰富，蛋白质含量达到15%左右。青稞的茎和叶又是家畜过冬的最好饲料。由于青稞品种、磨具、加工方式的不同，其种类和口感也不尽相同。青稞子经炒熟后研磨为粉状，称作"糌粑"，一直是人们的主食之一。制作时，先将青稞在沸水里煮洗后，闷上一个昼夜，再用火焙熟，加上少许花椒、黄果皮等香料，研磨成粉，和酥油茶一起捏成团后食用，口感极好，又易于消化。青稞酒则是当地人喜爱的白酒，用高原特有的青稞酿制而成。青稞酒酒色纯净，清香扑鼻，酒味绵软柔长。凡有客人临门，主人必敬青稞酒，并高唱一曲敬酒歌。青稞酒夏能提神，冬能驱寒，让人回味绵长。

（二）牦牛肉

牦牛是青藏高原独有的家畜之一，牦牛身躯高大，心、肺发达，肌肉紧凑，身长腿短，筋骨结实，腹部和四肢的皮毛柔软厚密。牦牛采食能力很强，能爬高山峭壁，可涉沼泽，可在冰上行走。它丰富的毛发和皮下组织可以帮助它在高寒低温下生活。牦牛全身上下都是宝，肉可食用，牛头可加工成工艺品，牛尾可以制作成扫帚。公牦牛多肉，母牦牛产奶。由于牦牛常年生活在海拔3 500米以上的地区，经常食用当地贝母、虫草等野生药材，所以牦牛肉及奶制品都是天然有机食品，营养成分丰富，肉味鲜美，受到美食家的追捧。牦牛宰杀后可红烧、清炖、晾晒成干巴等，其味道独特。牦牛肉刺身也是游客必挑战的美味之一，牦牛肉切成薄片，鲜滑不腥，搭配酱料入口，一定会让你终生难忘。

（三）酥油茶

酥油茶是当地人生活中不可或缺的饮品，其制作过程较为复杂，需将特制的茶叶煮沸，再在茶水中加上酥油、食盐、碾碎的核桃仁和麻子，最后用茶桶充分搅拌，这样制作出来的才是上好的酥油茶。香格里拉气候寒冷，酥油茶具有极高的热量，能驱寒提神。初尝酥油茶，第一口或许异味难耐，但再品，醇厚的酥油香和清香的茶叶，再加上捣碎的核桃，口感丰富，回味无穷。千百年来，人们创造了酥油茶文化，青年男女参加茶会活动，将交友、离别等情感寄托于酥油茶之中。

（四）冬虫夏草

在香格里拉海拔 4 000 米左右的雪山草甸上，生长着一种特殊的植物——冬虫夏草。虫草是一种真菌，一般在夏秋季节进入虫体，昆虫过冬期间，真菌在虫体内繁殖，第二年从虫体中长出杆状植株来。

冬虫夏草需手工采集，由于价格昂贵，使用它也被认为是身份的象征。由于特殊的构造，冬虫夏草一直都是各类研究的重点，但人工养殖仍没有投入商用。这也导致了其价格一直居高不下。然而，过度的开发导致冬虫夏草被列为易危物种。同时，由于连年对冬虫夏草资源的采集，草场退化严重，草地生态环境也逐渐恶化。我们需要做更多的研究，以了解其形态和生长习性，以便进行保护和最佳利用。

（五）松茸

松茸被称为"万菌之王"，香格里拉松茸以"菇体肥大，肉质细嫩，香久味浓,色泽好"而闻名中外,远销日本等国。松茸富含蛋白质、脂肪、粗纤维和维生素。松茸之所以珍贵还因为其对生长环境要求非常苛刻,只能存活在没有任何污染的原始森林中。松茸在出土前要有充足的雨水滋润,出土后必须有充足的阳光照射。而且气温、虫伤、人为不当方式采集等因素都会对松茸生长产生直接影响。松茸的生长十分缓慢,一般五六年才有可能产出松茸。而每年采摘松茸的季节只有七八月的雨季,松茸一旦长出,需要在三五天内采挖,才能保证其新鲜和营养。松茸的菌盖一旦散开,营养物质也就随着气味散开,松茸的价值便也打了折扣。松茸至今也无法人工培育,所以每一支松茸的诞生都是大自然的奇迹。

人们常说,高端的食材往往只需要采用最朴素的烹饪方式。生吃松茸口感新鲜,甚至有点刺激,还可以用松茸片蘸取芥末、酱油食用。平底锅小火融化适量黄油将松茸片煎至两面金黄,再撒上少许海盐和胡椒。松茸的食用方法很多,可以炖鸡、煮火锅,甚至还可以做成松茸饭、松茸茶。

Section Two　Food Culture—Gifts from the Plateau

The special natural geography and historical culture create a large number of local specialties in Shangri-La, such as highland barley, Cordyceps sinensis, matsutake mushrooms, Rhodiola, snow lotus and other natural specialties, as well as highland barley wine, butter tea, yak meat and so on.

Highland Barley

Highland barley is the most important food crop for the local people. It has a long cultivation history and a wide planting area. The seeds of highland barley are rich in nutrition, and the protein content reaches about 15%. The stems and leaves of highland barley are the best feed for livestock in winter.

Due to the different varieties, abrasives and processing methods, its types and tastes are also different. Highland barley seeds are ground into powder after frying, which is called "Zanba", and has always been one of the staple foods of the local. When cooking, the highland barley is boiled in boiling water, stuffy for a day and night, and then roasted with fire. With a little pepper, Huangguo peel and other spices, it is ground into powder, kneaded into a ball with butter tea, and then eaten. It tastes excellent and easy to digest. Highland barley wine is a Baijiu liquor that is very popular among the local people. Highland barley wine is pure in color, fragrant, and soft in taste. When guests come, the host will serve highland barley wine and sing a toast song. Highland barley wine can refresh the mind in summer and drive away the cold in winter, making people linger on the aftertaste.

Yak Meat

Yak is one of the unique livestock in the Qinghai-Tibet Plateau. Yak has a tall body, developed heart and lungs, compact muscles, short legs, strong muscles and bones, and is covered with soft and thick fur on its abdomen and limbs. Yaks are highly capable of feeding, climbing high mountain cliffs, wading in swamps and walking on ice. Its rich hair and subcutaneous tissue can help it live under high temperature and low temperature. No parts of yaks go waste. Their meat is edible, their heads can be processed into handicrafts and their tails can be made into brooms. The male yak is rich in meat and the female yak produces milk. They live in areas more than 3,500 meters above sea level all year round and often eat local fritillaria, cordyceps and other wild medicinal materials. Therefore, yak meat and dairy products are natural organic foods, rich in nutrients and delicious meat, which are sought after by gourmets. After slaughtered, yaks can be braised, stewed and dried, and they have unique tastes. Trying raw meat has also become a challenge for tourists. Sliced yak meat is fresh, smooth but not fishy. It will be unforgettable with the sauce.

Butter Tea

Butter tea is an indispensable drink for the local people. Its production process is relatively complex. In order to make the best butter tea, the special tea are boiled and added with butter, salt, crushed walnuts and hemp seeds, then the tea in the bucket is thoroughly stirred. Shangri-La has a cold climate, and butter tea has very high calorie, which can drive away the cold and refresh the mind. When you first taste butter tea, you may feel unbearable at first, but when you taste it again, the mellow butter aroma and fragrant tea, coupled with mashed walnuts, will give you a rich taste and endless aftertaste. For thousands of years, the local people have created butter tea culture and held tea parties for young men and women to attach their emotions such as making friends and parting in butter tea.

Cordyceps Sinensis

Cordyceps sinensis is a special plant growing on the snow mountain meadow in Shangri-La which is about 4,000 meters above sea level. Cordyceps sinensis is a kind of fungus, which usually enters the insect body in summer and autumn. During hibernation, the fungus propagates in the insect body and grows into rod-shaped plants from it the second year.

Cordyceps sinensis is collected by hand. Because of its high price, it is also considered as a symbol of identity. Due to its special structure, Cordyceps sinensis has always been the focus of various researches, but artificial cultivation has not been put into commercial use. This has also led to its high price. However, over exploitation has led to Cordyceps sinensis being classified as a "vulnerable" species. What's worse, due to the collection of Cordyceps sinensis resources year after year, the grassland has been seriously degraded and the grassland ecological environment has gradually deteriorated. We need to do more researches to understand its morphology and growth habits in order to protect and make the best use of it.

Matsutake

Matsutake is known as the "King of Mushrooms". Shangri-La matsutake is famous at home and abroad and is exported to Japan and other countries for its "large mushroom body, fine meat, lasting aroma, strong taste and good color". Matsutake is rich in protein, fat, crude fiber and vitamins. It is precious because it has very strict requirements for the growth environment and can only survive in the primary forest without any pollution. Matsutake should be moistened by sufficient rain before being unearthed, and must be exposed to sufficient sunshine after being unearthed. Moreover, temperature, insect injury, improper collection and other factors will have a direct impact on the growth of it. The growth of matsutake is very slow, and it generally takes 5 to 6 years. The annual season for picking it is only the rainy season from July to August. Once matsutake grows, it needs to be excavated within 3 to 5 days to ensure its freshness and nutrition. Once the cap of matsutake is dispersed, the nutrients will disperse with the smell, and the value will be decreased too. Matsutake can not be cultivated artificially, so the birth of each one is a miracle of nature.

People often use the simplest method to cook high-end ingredients. Raw matsutake tastes fresh and even a little stimulating. You can also dip sliced matsutake in mustard and soy sauce. Melt the butter in a saucepan over low heat, fry the matsutake slices until both sides turn golden, and then sprinkle a little sea salt and pepper. There are many ways to eat matsutake. It can be put in stewed chicken, hot pot, or even made into matsutake rice and matsutake tea.

> **Think and Discuss:**
> 2021年昆明举办的《生物多样性公约》第十五次缔约方大会上，松茸饼干成为嘉宾的伴手礼。而2020年，松茸首次被世界自然保护联盟列入世界濒危物种红色名录，我们应该如何做才能持续享用这道大自然的馈赠呢？

第三节　诗情画意 纳帕海湿地

纳帕海位于香格里拉市建塘镇，意为"森林背后的湖泊"。纳帕海不是"海"，且丰水期只有半年，但却是香格里拉最具代表性的原生态湿地。纳帕海位于多雨区与少雨区的过渡地带，年平均降水量 620 毫米，9 月至次年 5 月有雪。夏末秋初，雨水频降，再加上青龙潭、纳曲河、旺曲河水的注入，使得湖面大幅扩展、升高，水面最大时可达上千公顷①，于是便成了"海"。不过那时的纳帕海水流不深，牛或马可以随意蹚水而过，到岛中央的草地吃草、休憩。而旱季来临时，水面缩小，大部分地区便成为沼泽和草甸。

纳帕海保护区三面环山，地势平坦，自然气候湿润，所以这里的牧草比其他地方长得要快。每年的五六月份是纳帕海最美的季节，置身纳帕海之中，各种野花竞相开放，放眼望去，茫茫草原，牛羊成群，藏式村庄与巍峨雪山相得益彰，构成了极具视觉美感的画面，让人心神开阔。秋冬时节，转而金黄灿烂，远山如黛。

独特的环境和条件孕育了丰富的物种，也为横断山区南迁北徙的候鸟提供了舒适的越冬栖息地。每当秋季来临，草原一片金黄，皑皑雪峰倒映于湖泊之中。这一季节，黑颈鹤、黄鸭、斑头雁云集于此，在草丛中、水面上嬉戏漫游，在上空高飞低旋，堪称飞禽的乐园。使广阔空灵的草原另具一番诗情画意。

纳帕海在 2004 年被列为国际重要湿地，它是香格里拉的"绿肺"，也是人鸟的共同家园。不过，周围群众半农半牧的生活、城市的快速发展以及旅游业的发展都给纳帕海保护带来了压力。为了保护好纳帕海，当地管

---

① 1 公顷=0.01 平方千米。

委会实行"人退湖进"的总体策略,搬迁马场,拆除围栏,恢复退化湿地,以减少对湿地的侵扰。

Section Three　Poetic Painting—Napahai Wetland

　　Napahai is located in Jiantang Town, Shangri-La. It means "the lake behind the forest". Napahai is not a "sea", and the abundant water period is only half a year, but it is Shangri-La's most representative original ecological wetland. Napahai is located in the transitional zone between the pluvial and low-rain areas, with an average annual precipitation of 620 mm. The snow falls from September to May of the following year. At the end of summer and the beginning of autumn, rain drops frequently. With the injection of Qinglongtan, Naqu River and Wangqu River, the lake expands and rises sharply, and the water could reach thousands of hectares at its maximum, then it becomes the "sea". At that time, however, the water in Napahai is not deep, so the cattle and horses could wade through the water at will to the middle of the island to eat grass and take a rest. When the dry season comes, the water area is limited, and most areas become swamps and meadows.

　　The Napahai Reserve is surrounded by mountains on three sides, with a flat terrain and a wet natural climate, so grass here grows faster than anywhere else. The most beautiful season in Napahai is in May and June. At that time, you will see all kinds of wild flowers are in full bloom, and cattle and sheep roam at the vast prairie. Tibetan villages and towering snow mountains blend with each other, forming a very visual aesthetic picture, which makes people feel free. In autumn and winter, Napahai turns into golden yellow, and the mountains far away look gray and misty.

The unique environment and conditions not only bring rich species, but also provide a comfortable overwintering habitat for migratory birds moving south and north across the mountain area. When the autumn season comes, the prairie turns golden, and the snow-capped peaks reflect in the lakes. In this season, black-necked cranes, yellow ducks, spotted geese gather here, roam in the grass and on the surface of the water. They fly high and low in the sky. It can be called a paradise for birds which turns the vast and empty prairie into a poetic painting.

Napahai was listed as an international important wetland in 2004. It is the "green lung" of Shangri-La city, and it is also the common home of human and birds. However, the semi-agricultural and semi-pastoral life of the native, the rapid development of the city and tourism have all brought pressure to the protection of Napahai. In order to protect it, the local community is retreating the lake, moving the horse yard, demolishing the fence and restoring the degraded wetland in order to reduce the invasion of the wetland.

Think and Discuss:

内陆湖泊具有调节江河流量的作用，有利于生态平衡。1998年长江特大洪水期间，作为原来对长江洪水具有调节能力的洞庭湖、鄱阳湖和洪湖等湖泊，都因围湖造田而失去调节能力。请你结合你所了解的知识和信息，谈一谈退耕还湖的重要性。

第四节 奇秀悦目 普达措公园

普达措国家公园位于香格里拉市建塘镇红坡村,处于滇西北"三江并流"世界自然遗产中心地带,距香格里拉城区22千米,总面积约1 313平方千米,按7大板块进行开发,由国际重要湿地碧塔海自然保护区和"三江并流"世界自然遗产哈巴片区之属都湖景区两部分构成,以碧塔海、属都湖和弥里塘亚高山牧场为主要组成部分。普达措国家公园范围内最高点海拔4 670米,最低点海拔2 347米,有多处断层崖、林间小涧、深沟峡谷等独特小景交错分布,包含较为原始完整的森林灌丛、高山草甸、湿地湖泊、地质遗迹、河流峡谷生态系统等,具有较高的地理科学价值与旅游观赏价值。

(一)属都湖

属都湖隶属于普达措国家公园,离香格里拉市区35千米左右。属都湖水域面积达15平方千米,集高原湖泊、沼泽化草甸、原始暗针叶林植被于一身。湖中盛产属都裂腹鱼。鱼身金黄,腹部有一条裂纹,其肉质鲜嫩。属都湖四周青山郁郁,原始森林遮天蔽日,湖东面是成片的白桦树,秋天金黄遍野。

属都湖牧场是迪庆有名的牧场,草场广阔、水草丰茂,每年春夏之际,成群的牛羊漫步于湖畔,木棚星星点点,牧笛声声入耳,置身湖畔,让人深切感受到高原人恬静的生活。五六月是杜鹃花盛放的时期,漫山遍野的杜鹃花绽放在春日里,飘香四溢。入秋后,狼毒花竞相绽放,那一株株平时不太显眼的狼毒花此时便成为秋日里最浓墨重彩的一笔。

（二）碧塔海

相传天女梳妆时不小心失落的镜子破碎，形成许多高原湖泊，碧塔海就是其中一块镶有绿宝石的镜片。还有传说这里是《格萨尔王传》中提及的"毒湖"。又有人说这是明代丽江木天王的避暑地。在不远处的山上有一座庙宇。据说姜岭大战至碧塔海时，因冰天雪地，湖光朦胧，岭国的骑士们误入湖中而被淹没，转败为胜的姜国认为这是碧塔山神护佑的结果，便在小山上建造了庙宇。还有人说这是寻宝者建造的庙。

碧塔海水域面积1.65平方千米。平均水深20米，最深处达40米，素有"高原明珠"之称。沿着依山而建的栈道游览，两边植被茂密，绿荫密布，微风拂来，让人心旷神怡。晴天的碧塔海是最有风韵的，清澈的湖水在阳光映射下熠熠生辉，四周青山环抱，古木参天，倒映在湖水之中，如影如画。有云雾之时，湖面上烟波浩渺，一片朦胧，犹如在画中行走，如梦似幻。登高远望，湖的东南面和西北面是一片片草场，奇花异草，争奇斗艳。

"碧塔醉鱼"是碧塔海最著名的景观之一。湖的周围生长着浓密的杜鹃花林，每年农历五月，杜鹃盛开，花瓣纷纷飘落水中，常有游鱼吞食花瓣，因其含有微毒，鱼儿会如喝醉一般漂浮于水面，形成碧塔海一绝。

Section Four　Picturesque Scene—Pudacuo National Park

Pudacuo National Park is located in Hongpo village, Jiantang Town Shangri-La City. It is in the northwest of Yunnan and the center of The Three Parallel Rivers World Natural Heritage. It is 22 kilometers away from Shangri-La, with a total area of about 1,313 square kilometers. It consists of two parts: the Bita Lake Nature Reserve area and the Three Parallel Rivers

World Heritage Haba Lake Scenic Area. Bita Lake, Shudu Lake and Militang sub-alpine pastures are the three main components. The highest point of Pudacuo National Park is 4,670 meters above sea level, while the lowest elevation is 2,347 meters. A number of fault cliffs, streams, deep valleys and other unique scenery are staggeredly distributed in the national park. It also contains relatively primitive forests and shrubs, alpine meadows, wet lakes, geological relics, rivers, valleys and so on. Pudacuo National Park is the place with high geographical science value and tourism ornamental value.

Shudu Lake

Shudu Lake is located in the Pudacuo National Park, and is about 35 kilometers from Shangri-La. The water area of the lake is 15 square kilometers. It contains plateau lake, swamp meadow and the original dark coniferous forest vegetation. The lake abounds in "Liefuyu"(fish with cracks on their bellies). The body of this fish is golden, and there is a stripe in the belly. The meat is fresh and tender. The green hills are all around the lake and the forest blocks the sky. There are silver birches in the east of the lake, and they all turn yellow in autumn.

Shudu Lake pasture, with vast grassland and lush water plants, is one of the famous pasture in Diqing. In every spring and summer, the pasture is dotted with wooden sheds, and flocks of cattle and sheep walk in the lakeside. We can also hear the sound of the flute. The quiet life of plateau can be deeply felt by people there. May and June is the time when azaleas are in full bloom. All over the mountains and plains are carpeted with azaleas blossoms. The air is fragrant with sweet smell. In the autumn, the Langdu flowers bloom. Although Langdu flower is quite common in other time, it becomes the most outstanding scenery in autumn.

Bita Lake

Legend has it that when the goddess was dressing, the mirror dropped and shattered accidentally, then it became many plateau lakes. Bita Lake is the one inlaid with emeralds. It is also said the lake is the "Poison Lake" mentioned in *The Legend of King Gesar*. Some people say that it is the Chieftain Mu's summer resort in Ming Dynasty. And there is a temple in the near hill. When Jiang Ling War extended to Bita Lake, because of the icy world and hazy lake, Ling Kingdom's knights were drown in the Lake. Jiang Kingdom, who turned defeat into victory, believed that this was the result of the blessing of the Bita Mountain God and built a temple on the hill. Others say the temple was built by treasure hunters.

The water area of Bita Lake is 1.65 square kilometers. The average depth is 20 meters, the deepest is nearly 40 meters, and it is known as the Plateau Pearl. Walking in the plank road along the mountain, the breeze blowing, you will feel refreshed because of the dense vegetation and shade on both sides. The sunny days of Bita Lake is the most charming days. The clear water shines under the sun, and is surrounded by green mountains. It is such a picturesque place with the towering old trees reflected in the lake. When there are clouds, the mist on the lake is vast and hazy, as if you were walking in the painting. Seen from the hill, the southeast and northwest of the lake are patches of grassland and the flowers are colorful and blossomy.

Bita Drunk Fish is one of the most famous scenery in Bita Lake. There is a sea of azaleas around the lake. Every year in May of the lunar calendar, azaleas are in full bloom. Petals fall in the water, and are often swallowed by swimming fish. Because it contains micro-toxic substances, the fish will float on the water as if they were drunk, which become a unique scene in Bita Lake.

Think and Discuss:

1872年,世界上第一个国家公园——美国黄石国家公园建立,它是自然环境保护制度的先驱之一。到目前为止,全世界已有200多个国家建立了国家公园,而普达措国家公园是中国首批10个国家公园体制试点之一,请思考国家公园的建立有何意义?

第五节 鸟兽乐园 香格里拉

香格里拉市是鸟兽的乐园,它们在这里栖息觅食,嬉戏玩耍。引颈高歌的黑颈鹤、阔步前进的紫水鸟、洁白如雪的大白鹭、绿翅鸭、斑头雁,以及高原秃鹫等,或翩翩翱翔于天际,或栖息跳跃于水草之间,或在水中嬉戏追逐。337种鸟类为香格里拉的观鸟摄影旅游、生态旅游注入了新的活力,让人们逐渐了解了香格里拉本地鸟类资源和生物多样性。

(一) 黑颈鹤

黑颈鹤是国家一级保护动野生鸟类,仅分布在青藏高原和云贵高原,是世界上唯一的一种生长、繁殖在高原的鹤类。1876年,俄国探险家第一次在中国青海湖发现黑颈鹤,这是全球发现得最晚的一种鹤类,使世界鹤类总数达到15种。

每年入冬时节,黑颈鹤从青海湖等地陆续飞抵香格里拉。由于纳帕海水草丰茂,能提供黑颈鹤的食物——黄蚬、小鱼、植物根茎、水草及蝌蚪等,且少有人迹毁坏环境,气候适宜,故而成了黑颈鹤理想的栖息地。纳帕海自然保护区是一个天然湖泊,这里草肥水美,保护完好的原生态环境吸引了黑颈鹤每年冬季前来栖息。成群结队的黑颈鹤或起飞滑翔,或翩翩起舞,或悠然漫步,与人和睦相处,虚幻而又真实,令人心旷神怡。

在当地,流传着一个动人的传说:很久以前,黑颈鹤经常到青稞地中寻觅青稞种子,到青稞长出后又大吃青稞苗,待到秋天青稞成熟时则啄食青稞籽。人们对黑颈鹤又气又无奈,最终想办法扣住了它。人与鹤都想和平共处,于是双方结为兄弟,定下盟约:黑颈鹤永远不再破坏庄稼,只吃危害庄稼的害虫;人类永远不再捕杀黑颈鹤,并将自己的三根头发给了黑颈鹤，要它装点在头部以证明与人类的亲情。从此，黑颈鹤的头上就出现了三根人的头发。从这个故事可以看到人类和黑颈鹤和谐共处的良好关系及美好愿景。

（二）滇金丝猴

滇金丝猴是中国特有的珍稀濒危灵长类动物。滇金丝猴是国家一级保护动物，主要分布在滇西北和藏东南一带的高寒原始森林，被誉为"雪山精灵"，也是世界自然保护联盟红色名录中的濒危物种。

滇金丝猴栖息于海拔3 000米以上的高山暗针叶林带，活动范围在2 500米到5 000米的高山，以竹笋、植物的嫩叶、嫩芽和花苞等为食。初生的幼仔全身的皮毛为浅黄色，两眼大而有神，四肢的趾尖都是红色，口唇则呈樱桃红，就像涂了口红的少女一般。

20世纪80年代前后，打猎和伐木等行为对滇金丝猴栖息地造成了破坏，猴群数量一度减少，保护形势严峻。为了拯救濒危的滇金丝猴，中国建立了香格里拉白马雪山自然保护区。曾经对生态造成破坏的村民，也逐渐加入保护当地生态环境的队伍中，成为保护区的护猴员。经过多年的努力，滇金丝猴保护成效明显。滇金丝猴的保护成效可以说是我国持续推动生物多样性治理和生态文明建设的生动例证。

Section Five Paradise for Birds and Animals—Shangri-La

Shangri-La is a paradise for birds and animals, where they can perch and play freely. Black-necked cranes, purple water birds, snowy white egrets, green-winged ducks, bar-headed geese and highland vultures fly in the sky, jump between the grass, and chase in the water. 337 species of birds re-energize the Shangri-La bird-watching photography, tourism and eco-tourism development, so people can gradually understand the local bird resources and biodiversity in Shangri-La.

Black-Necked Crane

Black-necked crane is the class A national protected animal. It is distributed in the Qinghai-Tibet Plateau and Yunnan-Guizhou Plateau, and the only kind of crane growing and breeding in the plateau in the world. In 1876, Russian explorers discovered black-necked cranes in China's Qinghai Lake for the first time, which is the latest crane discovered in the world. Therefore, the total number of cranes' types in the world reached 15.

Black-necked cranes fly from Qinghai Lake and other places to Shangri-La every winter. Due to the abundance of aquatic plants in the Napahai, it provides food for the black-necked cranes, such as yellow clams, small fish, plant roots, aquatic plants and tadpoles. Meanwhile, because of few human activities and suitable climate, it has become an ideal habitat for the black-necked crane. Napahai is a natural lake, where the grass is fertile, the water is clear, and the original ecological environment is well preserved, which attracts black-necked cranes to come to live in winter every year. Groups of black-necked cranes live in harmony with people, gliding, dancing and strolling, which makes it an unreal picture for us.

There is a touching legend in the local area. Long time ago, black-necked cranes often ate barley seeds. When seeds grew up, they ate seedlings. In the autumn when the barley matured, they peck barley seeds again. The people were angry and helpless with the black-necked crane, and finally caught them. Man and the crane wanted to live together peacefully, so they became brothers and made a promise: the black-necked crane would never destroy crops again, but only eat pests that harm crops; humans would never kill the black-necked crane, and give the crane three of people's hair to decorate their heads in order to prove their love with humans. Since then, three human hairs have appeared on the black-necked crane's head. From this story, we can see the good relationship and beautiful vision of the harmonious coexistence of humans and black-necked cranes.

Yunnan Snub-Nosed Monkey

Yunnan snub-nosed monkey is a rare and endangered primate in China. Yunnan snub-nosed monkey is a national first-class protected animal, mainly distributed in the alpine primeval forests of Northwest Yunnan and Southeast Tibet. It is known as the "Snow Mountain Elf", and is also an endangered species on the IUCN Red List.

Yunnan snub-nosed monkey inhabits the alpine dark coniferous forest zone, which is 3,000 meters above sea level. The range of activities can be from 2,500 meters to 5,000 meters high mountain. Bamboo shoots, plant leaves, buds and flower buds are the main food to the monkey. The newborn pups have pale yellow fur, big eyes, red toes, and cherry red lips, just like a girl with lipstick.

Around the 1980s, hunting and logging activities damaged the habitat of Yunnan snub-nosed monkey, which led to the number of monkey groups reducing dramatically. The situation was grim. In order to save the endangered Yunnan snub-nosed monkey, China has established the Shangri-la Baima Snow Mountain natural conservation area. The villagers, who once damaged environment, have gradually joined to protect the local ecology and become the monkey protectors of the conservation area. After years of efforts, the protection effect of Yunnan snub-nosed monkey is obvious, The conservation of Yunnan snub-nosed monkey can be said to be a vivid example of China's continuous promotion of biodiversity management and ecological development.

> **Think and Discuss:**
> 香格里拉有很多珍稀的动植物。过去,人类为了生存和发展,不断地侵扰动植物的生存空间。在人与自然的关系中,人类处于主动的地位。请思考在现代社会中人与动物应该如何共存。

第六节　创艺之美　香格里拉

除了雄壮洁白的雪山、纵横交错的山谷、广阔丰沛的草甸，香格里拉人民在悠久的历史长河中也创造了丰富多彩的手工艺品，成为这片土地上的文化瑰宝。随着经济的快速发展，当地人民的生活渐渐远离了这些传统制品，但近年来，外地游客及人们观念的改变，使很多民间手工艺品重新受到了人们的追捧。香格里拉的民间手工艺品具有古朴、粗犷、自然之美，符合现代人返璞归真、崇尚自然的环保理念和审美取向。

（一）尼西黑陶

香格里拉尼西乡的村民们几千年来一直制作着一种黑色的陶器。据传3000多年前，人们已经开始制作夹砂褐陶器，其器形属于寺洼文化。时间虽已过数千年，香格里拉尼西石棺中出土的黑陶颜色依然黝黑，其器形简单，主要是锅、壶、罐等生活用具。从19世纪中叶开始，其工艺更加成熟，能够生产酥油茶罐、土火锅、土砂锅等多种陶器。在金属制品尚未被当地人民使用之前，黑陶制品可以说是最奢侈的生活用品。因此，尼西火锅远近闻名。用其烹制食物，味道鲜美，让人垂涎欲滴，又因为是天然陶土制作，对人体无害，备受当地人民喜爱。2008年，陶器烧制技艺入选第二批国家级非物质文化遗产代表性名录。

尼西黑陶主要由当地特有的红土和白土混合而成，碾碎后掺入风化石，经过备料、塑形、雕花、阴干、烧制等工序，最终形成陶体漆黑、光洁细腻的独特陶艺制品。尼西黑陶在制作时不搭建窑炉，而是在露天生起一堆篝火，依次将陶器摆放在底架上烧制，期间，还需要不断地在柴堆周围加木材以助燃。由于大量的锯木粉使得烧制的火堆内缺氧，烧成后的陶瓷就被熏成了黑色。

现在，由于当地人对传统工艺的重视以及旅游业的发展，越来越多的年轻人开始学习制陶手艺，原始的制陶业在今天得到了前所未有的发展，成为当地的一大产业。与此同时，在保留传统工艺的基础上，当地也开始适时进行创新和变革。通过不断改善黑陶泥土的配比方案，使黑陶在外形和质量上达到最佳，一些地方开始使用电窑烧制，使陶器适应了现代生活高温烹制的要求。在当地烧陶人看来，古老守旧的烧制方式可以改变，笨重的器皿样式也可以创新。为了适应新的生活环境及满足游客要求，黑陶增加了许多新的工艺品，如花瓶、酒杯、烟灰缸等，其工艺也越来越精致，兼具实用性和观赏价值。

（二）木碗

香格里拉人民在日常生活中习惯使用传统木制品的用具，如木碗、木盒、糌粑盒等，其造型古朴典雅，而其中使用最为普遍的便是当地的特色木碗。很多当地人都有使用自己专属木碗的习惯，例如用来盛放酥油茶的小碗、用来装糌粑的大碗、用来放酥油的盖碗以及用来放佐料的套碗。父母会为新生的孩子准备精致的木碗，伴随孩子一生，故此，香格里拉甚至有"一人一碗，一碗一生"的说法。木碗寄相思，丈夫远行，妻子会将双方的碗倒满茶，饮尽自己的茶，再将丈夫的茶倒在地上，收好木碗，等待丈夫回归。由此可见木碗在当地人心中的分量。

杜鹃根、核桃木、柳木等都是用于制作木碗的原材料。上等的木碗需选用蒿枝根部寄生的一种瘤作原料，其木质光滑、细腻，纹路细致、清晰。由于蒿枝瘤较难获得，因此这种木碗便成了精品。木碗制作要经过选料、晾干、做毛坯、水煮、修整成型、上漆等多道工序。制成的木碗，一套三个，两大一小，两个大碗可将小碗扣合于其中形成一个扁圆的"木球"，十分精巧。人们使用木碗也很有讲究，男女所用样式不同，男式木碗碗口

大且外开，碗身低；女式木碗则恰好相反，开口较小，碗身较细。许多人家还给木碗包上了银边，碗上刻有吉祥图案，有的碗盖还镶有玛瑙等装饰品。

香格里拉上桥头村因生产木碗而闻名，这里的木碗制作历史可以追溯到200多年前。过去，村子是茶马古道的要冲，来来往往的马帮运送普洱茶、日用品，把当地的木碗、糌粑盒带去西藏。香格里拉人民多以从事畜牧业为主，木碗轻巧便于携带，不易破碎，因此，制作使用木碗的习俗便沿袭了下来。为了传播木碗文化，当地的非遗传承人还在当地农家院中开展了漆器体验项目，有许多的外地人到这里拜师学艺。如今，这项传统的制作工艺成为很多农户的致富产业。

（三）卡卓刀

卡卓刀是香格里拉久负盛名的传统工艺之一，其精美的外观和浓郁的文化特色，让卡卓刀成为游客争相收藏的艺术品。卡卓刀广泛应用于当地群众生活的方方面面。卡卓意味"平安、吉祥、长命百岁"。"卡卓"是家族的姓氏，其家族世代以打铁为生，经过一百多年的传承，卡卓家族研制出了一套锻造刀剑的鏊钢药水，炼制出了削铁如泥的刀剑，后代子孙还把自己打刀的心得记入刀谱世代相传，使得卡卓刀闻名于香格里拉、西藏等地区。

卡卓刀造型精美，刀身以银为主要材料，男士刀比较粗犷，女式则较为秀气。卡卓刀可作为切肉的餐具，还可以作为特殊的装饰品。其独特的锻造、淬火工艺和药水配兑秘方，为卡卓刀的整体强度和冲击耐受力提供了强有力的保证，卡卓刀锋利耐用。刀身图案以传统文化图腾为设计理念，其刀鞘和刀柄锚金错银，镶嵌着玛瑙、珊瑚和绿松石，精细雕刻着藏八宝、大鹏鸟、麒麟等吉祥图案，使其显得格外华丽和精美。

如今，卡卓品牌系列藏刀在传承历史的基础上不断吸收新的营养，从过去家庭作坊式的生产模式发展成集刀具、工艺品生产、加工、销售为一体的知名企业。卡卓公司一方面加强对传统制刀工艺的研究开发，不断改进生产工艺技术，提高卡卓刀具的品质；另一方面挖掘香格里拉民间制刀人才，经过系统的培训后进行卡卓刀的生产，扩大了卡卓刀的影响力和知名度，同时也将传统文化传播到了更远的地方。2007年5月，为进一步加强卡卓刀文化的保护与传承，香格里拉还建立了集藏刀收藏、研究、展示、教育、宣传等功能为一体的迪庆州卡卓刀文化博物馆，让更多人对藏刀这一传统文化有了更深的认识。

香格里拉传统的技艺和文化在历史的长河中绵延了上千年，而现在，也正以一种悄然无息的方式融进了人们的生活中。无论社会如何变迁，香格里拉的传统技艺正在以其自身的方式适应着社会的发展、人类的进步，焕发出新的光彩。

Section Six　　The Beauty of Crafts

In addition to the majestic white snow mountains, crisscrossed valleys and broad meadows in Shangri-La, in the long history, the people there have also created a variety of handicrafts, which have become the cultural treasures of this land. Due to the rapid development of the local economy, these traditional products were gradually put away by local people. But in recent years, many folk handicrafts regained popularity due to the change of tourists' and people's perception. Shangri-La folk handicrafts are simple, rough and natural, which are in line with modern people's concept and aesthetic orientation of backing to nature and advocating natural environmental protection at the same time.

Black Pottery of Nixi

The villagers of Nixi, Shangri-La, have been making Black Pottery for thousands of years. It is said that more than 3,000 years ago, people have begun to make sand-lined brown pottery which belongs to the Si Wa culture. Although thousands of years have passed, the Black Pottery unearthed in Shangri-La Nixi sarcophagus is still dark in color and simple in shape. Most of them are pots and other living utensils. Since the middle of the 19th century, its technology has become more mature, and it can produce a variety of pottery, such as butter tea pots, hot pot, and casseroles. Before metal products were used by the local people, Black Pottery products were the most luxurious daily necessities. Therefore, Nixi hot pot is famous for its delicious taste and mouth-watering food, and because the pot is made of natural clay, it is harmless to the human and loved by the local people. In 2008, pottery firing techniques were selected into the Second Batch of National Intangible Cultural Heritage representative list.

Nixi Black Pottery is mainly made of a mixture of local red earth and clay. After grinding weathering, preparation, shaping, carving, shady drying, firing and other processes, it finally forms black, smooth, delicate and unique pottery products. Rather than building a kiln, Nixi Black Pottery was made in an open area, with the pottery placed on a base and constantly adding wood around the pyre for combustion. The large amount of sawdust leads to the lack of oxygen in fire, and finally smokes the pot into black.

Now, due to the local people's attention to traditional crafts and the development of tourism, more and more young people begin to learn pottery making, and the primitive pottery industry has seen unprecedented development and has become a major industry in the region. At the same time, on the basis of retaining traditional skills, local innovation and change are also applied. Through the continuous improvement of the proportion of black pottery soil, the shape and quality of black pottery achieved the best, and some places began to use electric kiln firing, which made pottery adapt to the requirements of high temperature cooking in modern life. In the eyes of the local potters, the old and conservative firing method can be changed, and the heavy pottery style can also be innovated. In order to adapt to the new living environment and meet the requirements of tourists, there are more new crafts added into Black Pottery, such as vases, wine glasses, ashtrays, etc., and its technology is becoming more and more delicate, with both practical and ornamental value.

Wooden Bowls

The people of Shangri-La are accustomed to using traditional wooden utensils in their daily lives, such as wooden bowls, wooden boxes, tsampa boxes, etc., which are of primitive simplicity and elegance. Among them, the most commonly used is the local special wooden bowl. Many locals have the habit of using their own exclusive wooden bowl. For example, a small bowl for holding butter tea, a large bowl for carrying tsampa, a covered bowl for putting butter, and a set bowl for placing seasoning. Parents will prepare exquisite wooden bowls for their newborn children, accompanying the children for a whole life. Therefore, there is a saying "one bowl for one person, a bowl for life" in Shangri-La. The wooden bowl carries the lovesickness. When the husband travels far, the wife will pour the bowl of both sides full of tea, and drink her own tea off, then pour the husband's tea and put the wooden bowl away, waiting for the husband to return. This shows the importance of the wooden bowl among the local people.

Azalea root, walnut, willow, etc. are raw materials used to make wooden bowls. The superior wooden bowl needs a kind of tumor parasitic on the root of the wormwood. Its wood is smooth, delicate, fine and with clear lines.

Because the wormwood is difficult to obtain, this wooden bowl has become a boutique. Wooden bowl production goes through material selection, drying, rough casting, boiling, molding, painting and other processes. The wooden bowls are always grouped by a set of three, with two large ones and a small one. Those two big bowls can be buckled in to form a delicate oblate "wooden ball". People are very particular about the use of wooden bowls. Men's style is different from women's. Men's wooden bowls are large and open, and the bowl is low; on the contrary, women's bowl is small and thin. Many families also bound silver edge on the bowl, engraved with auspicious patterns. Some bowl covers are inlaid with agate and other decorations.

Shangqiaotou Village is famous for its wooden bowls. The history can be dated to 200 years ago. The village was the fortress of the ancient Tea-Horse Road. Caravans transported Pu'er tea, daily necessities, local wooden bowls and zanba boxes to Tibet. People in Shangri-La are mainly engaged in animal husbandry, and the wooden bowl is easy to carry since it's light and not easy to break. Therefore, the custom of making and using wooden bowls has been handed down. In order to spread the wooden bowl culture, the local intangible cultural heritage inheritors carry out lacquerware experience projects in the local farmyard, and many outsiders come here to learn. Today, this traditional craft has become an industry for locals to make a better life.

The Kazhuo Knife

The Kazhuo knife is one of Shangri-La's most prestigious traditional crafts. Its exquisite appearance and rich cultural characteristics make it a popular art collection for tourists. Kazhuo knives are also widely used in all aspects of local people's lives. Kazhuo means "peace, good luck and long life". "Kazhuo" is a family name, and this family made a living as blacksmith for generations. After more than 100 years of inheritance, the Kazhuo family developed a set of potions for forging sharp steel sword and knife. Future generations also recorded their own experience in notes, making Kazhuo knife famous in Shangri-La, Tibet and other regions.

Kazhuo knife is exquisite in shape and mainly made of silver. Men's knife can be rough, while women's is delicate. Kazhuo knives can be used for cutting meat, or as special decorations. Its unique forging, quenching process and secret recipe provide a strong guarantee for the strength and impact resistance to Kazhuo knife, making it sharp and durable. The design of the body is based on the traditional culture totem. Inlaid with agate, coral and turquoise, Kazhuo knife is finely carved with Tibetan eight treasures, bird, Kylin and other auspicious patterns, making it particularly gorgeous and luxurious.

Nowadays, Kazhuo brand constantly absorbs new ideas on the basis of inherited history. It has become a well-known enterprise combining knife and handicraft production, processing and sales. On the one hand, the company strengthens the research and development of traditional knife making technology, continuously improves the production technology and the quality of Kazhuo knife. On the other hand, they search for the folk knife talents in Shangri-La, and carry out the production after systematic training. It not only expands the influence and popularity of Kazhuo knife, but also spreads the traditional culture to more distant places. In May 2007, in order to strengthen the protection and inheritance of the Tibetan knife culture, Shangri-La established the Diqing State Kazhuo knife Culture Museum, which integrates the collection, research, display, education and publicity of Tibetan knives. It lets more people have a deeper understanding of the traditional culture of Tibetan knife.

The traditional skills and culture in Shangri-La have passed down for thousands of years. And now, they are also incorporated into people's lives quietly. No matter how the society changes, Shangri-La's traditional skills are adapting to the development of society and the progress of mankind in their own way.

Think and Discuss:

1. 香格里拉有很多特色手工艺品，你们家乡有什么传统的文化和工艺品？请分享一下它们以及它们蕴含的历史记忆与文化内涵。

2. 在科技发展速度如此之快的今天，很多传统工艺都已经失传，作为年轻人，我们应该如何为传统文化艺术的推广和传承贡献自己的力量呢？

第六章　其他篇[①]
Chapter VI　Charming Places In Yunnan

第一节　千年古城建水

云南边陲有这样一座国家级历史文化名城,它有1 200余年的建城历史,拥有国家级非物质文化遗产"中国四大名陶"之一的民间传统工艺品,这便是2019年被授予"中国紫陶之都"的云南建水县。如今的紫陶街已变成热闹非凡的旅游打卡地。街道两旁的传统紫陶店铺配上现代的酒吧、电影院、小吃店,实现了传统温度与商业热度的良好均衡,为游客探寻这座千年古城提供了舒适的场景。

说到建水,美食"三叠水"不能缺席,它是滇南饮食文化的代表,是当地人招待宾客的最高礼仪。"三叠水"菜式丰富,上菜三套,又被称为"三叠水宴"。"一叠"是甜品,好吃养生,4个小杯盛有桂圆莲子汤、大枣冰糖水、紫米稀饭、燕窝汤;4个小碟装有小块蛋酥、金钱酥、火腿酥和狮子糕。"二叠"是主食,共有24道菜。上菜时每次上8道菜,浓淡搭配,分3次上完。"三叠"是水果,有梨、桃、橘子等8种水果。可谓菜品应有尽有,营养均衡搭配至极。这道菜彰显的不仅是当地人的饮食智慧,更是多少宾客难带走、藏心底的舌尖味道。

[①] 资料来源:云南红河建水美食"三叠水". 冯水芳. 建水融媒号,"学习强国",2021年07月12日,摘自2022年05月02日。

Section One　The Thousand-Year Ancient Town—Jianshui County

　　In the border of Yunnan locates a national historical and cultural town with a long history of 1,200 years. It is Jianshui county, the capital of China's traditional folk purple pottery handicraft (awarded in 2019), which is one of China's four famous potteries and has been listed as the national intangible cultural heritage. The present purple pottery street has become a famous resort place bustling with modern bars, movie theaters, snack food bars and traditional purple pottery shops on its two sides, which achieves a harmonious balance between the traditional culture and modern commercial, offering tourists a good place to explore this ancient town.

　　Speaking of Jianshui, the local cuisine—Sandieshui must be talked about. It represents the cuisine culture of the south of Yunnan and is the highest etiquette to welcome guests. The cuisine, for its rich dishes, usually three courses, is also called "Sandieshui Banquet". The first course (also known as "yidie") is tasteful and nutritional dessert composed of four small bowls of longan and lotus seed soup, crystal sugar soup with Chinese dates, purple rice congee, and swifts' nest soup respectively, and four small dishes of egg souffle, jinqian souffle, ham souffle and shizi cake respectively; the second course (also known as "erdie") is staple food consisting of 24 dishes balanced in meat and vegetables, which are served three times, 8 dishes once; the third course (also known as "sandie") is constituted of 8 kinds of fruits such as pears, peaches and oranges, etc. Sandieshui cuisine, for its rich content and balanced nutrition, epitomizes the local people's wisdom and thus has won many tourists' tongue and hearts.

第二节 水乡玉溪[①]

玉溪因水得名，有清流如玉之意。坐拥飞瀑流泉，面朝深泽大湖。抚仙湖、星云湖、杞麓湖，独占云南省"九大高原湖泊"中的三席，它们如同三颗明珠装点着玉溪，滋养着玉溪。

有着诗一样名字的抚仙湖是地球上同一纬度地区水质保持最好的淡水湖泊。抚仙湖水质好，湖水清澈，风光极佳。以抚仙湖为核心的湖景美不胜收，已成为全国少有的户外体育运动天堂与休闲康养度假旅游目的地。

玉溪境内的哀牢山是全球同纬度生物多样性、同类型植物群落保留最完整的地区，物种多样，动植物资源丰富，森林覆盖率达71.5%，1 016种高等植物、460多种野生动物在这里繁衍生息，成就了天然的自然博物馆。

水乡玉溪也是一座历史的博物馆，承载着一座城市过去的记忆。这里是中国唯一化石类世界自然遗产澄江帽天山古生物化石群的故乡；这里的江川甘棠箐旧石器遗址发掘出土的木制品是迄今为止世界上发现最早的木制品，再次证明了滇中高原是人类起源的关键区域；这里的江川李家山出土的"牛虎铜案"与甘肃的"马踏飞燕"被誉为中国青铜艺术圣殿的"双璧"；这里有被誉为云南四大名山的通海秀山，至今还悬挂着200余副楹联；这里的玉溪青花瓷、华宁陶、通海银、江川铜等非遗技艺薪火相传，使玉溪文脉源远流长。

[①] 资料来源：云南玉溪：高原水乡 清流如玉. 谷朋，李晶晶，念新洪. 云南学习平台，"学习强国"，2019年06月10日，摘自2022年05月02日.
云南省弥勒市：把城市空间留给市民. 人民日报，"学习强国"，2022年07月29日，摘自2022年08月01日.

Section Two   Yuxi—a Water City

Yuxi, a name related to water, implying the beauty of jade-like clear water. The waterfalls, springs and lakes on this land, especially the three lakes of Yunnan nine plateau lakes, Fuxian Lake, Xingyun Lake and Qilu Lake, like three pearls, have been decorating and nourishing Yuxi.

Fuxian Lake, with a poetic name, is a freshwater lake with the best preserved water quality of the same altitude on earth. Except for its good quality water, the scenery here is also magnificent. The area centering around Fuxian Lake has become the national outdoor sports heaven and the tourist resort for leisure and healthcare.

The Ailao Mountain in Yuxi is the area owning the best preserved biological diversity of the same altitude in the world and the plant community of the same category, which creates various species and rich resources of animals and plants. The forest cover rate here is up to 71.5% and here is the home to 1,016 kinds of advanced plants and 460 kinds of wild animals, which give Yuxi the title of a natural museum of nature.

Yuxi is also a museum of history, which stores the past memory of this city and records its civilization, In this museum of history, there is the Maotianshan ancient biological fossil community in Dengjiang county, the only world natural heritage of fossils in China; there is the Gantangjing Paleolithic sites in Jiangchuan, where the world earliest wooden products were excavated, the strong evidence that the central part of Yunnan is the pivotal area of human origin; there is the "Ox-tiger bronze case" excavated in Lijiashan, Jiangchuan, together with the "Horse with one swallow under its foot" excavated in Gansu, are considered the two most representative and historically significant bronze crafts of China; there is the Xiu mountain in Tonghai county, one of the four most famous mountains in Yunnan especially for its 200 couplets; there are also rich handicrafts as intangible heritage such as Yuxi blue-and-white porcelain, Huaning pottery, Tonghai silverware and Jiangchuan bronze, which are carried forward from one generation to another, making the long-standing memory of this city's history and culture.

第三节　山水田城弥勒[①]

有这样一座滇南小城，把城市的美丽空间留给了它的居民，它便是山水田城——弥勒。本着"还河于民"的治理原则，弥勒市完成了 8.3 千米的河道治理，形成了融生态廊道、湿地公园、旅游休闲一体的城市生态空间。如今地处高原的弥勒，甸溪河畔，白鹭展翅，椰树成行，岸堤廊道，草木茂盛，市民与游客徜徉其间，心旷神怡。车水马龙的弥勒市区，建起了大大小小的"口袋公园"。浓密的柳荫下，浮萍随风而动；磊磊山石旁，一株株紫棉木、枫树挺拔生长。入夜，皓月当空，夏虫低鸣，湖泉生态园里，沿着湖堤漫步、夜跑的人三五成群、夜钓的人三三两两，在享受着闲适、自得的城市生活。

弥勒亲水，更亲人。这座滇南小城在变绿，市民的宜居空间也在不断扩大。全市森林覆盖率达 50%，绿色已成为弥勒市高质量发展最耀眼的底色。目前，这座滇南小城正成为热门旅游目的地。城区的海棠花尽情绽放，粉红的花儿开满枝头，引来蜂舞鸟鸣，春风吹过，飘出淡淡芳香，"一时开处一城香"的诗意景象呈现在游人眼前。

Section Three　Mile—a Park-Like City

In the south of Yunnan, there is a small city, which builds a beautiful park-like homeland for its citizens. It is Mile, a city like a park. Based on the

---

① 资料来源：云南弥勒：打造绿色韵味 亮出耀眼底色. 李昱廷，弥勒融媒号，"学习强国"，2022 年 06 月 05 日，摘自 2022 年 07 月 01 日。

principle of "returning rivers to the people", the city has completed the river regulation of 8.3 kilometers, creating urban ecological space that is integrated with ecological corridors, wetland parks, tourism and leisure. Wandering in this city located in the plateau, citizens and tourists feel relaxed and happy by enjoying the Dianxi River lined with coconut trees on its bank corridors, the egrets flying, and grass and trees flourishing. In the busy downtown area, many "pocket parks" have been built, large or small. Under the dense willow shade, duckweed moves with the wind; next to the piles of rocks, purple cotton trees and maple trees grow tall and straight. When night falls, the bright moon hanging high in the sky and the summer insects chirping, people in the Huquan Ecological Park start their leisure and laid-back city life, some walking along the lake bank, some jogging in groups and some fishing by twos and threes.

The municipality of Mile pays special attention to the environment and attaches more importance to the quality of people's lives, therefore, this small city in Southern Yunnan is becoming greener, and the livable space for citizens is thus expanding. The forest coverage rate of the city has reached 50%, and green has become the most dazzling background color for its high-quality development. Living on the land of home, also the current popular tourist destination, people are enjoying their happiness to the fullest. In the urban area, the Chinese flowering apple is blooming, with the pink flowers covering the branches, drawing the buzzing bees and chirping birds. When the spring breeze blows, light fragrance floats in the air, and the poetic scene of "One tree blossoms, and the whole city is fragrant" unfolds before the visitors.

第四节 茶乡普洱①

说到云南普洱，不得不提及普洱茶。作为普洱茶的主产地之一，来到普洱，一定得品一品这岁月抚摸过的芳华。

中国是世界上最早发现及饮用茶叶的国家。中国茶类繁多，只有普洱茶以一隅之地而闻名天下，被誉为世界茶源。通过自然的积淀与时间的打磨，品质优良的普洱茶才会孕育而生。根据加工工艺的不同，普洱茶有生茶和熟茶之分。2008年，普洱茶制作技艺（贡茶制作技艺与大益普洱茶制作技艺）入选第二批国家级非物质文化遗产名录。品饮普洱茶，品的不仅是云南地区的山光水色，更是品饮云南特色文化的独特风味。在我国六大茶山之一的普洱景迈山，拥有名扬四海的古树茶。冬季，在那里还可以同时欣赏到日出与云海，品茶赏景，难得同时拥有。

茶乡普洱也是咖啡的种植地，具有得天独厚的种植条件。目前，普洱市已经成为全国种植面积最大、产量最高、品质最优的咖啡主产区和咖啡贸易的主要集散点。一茶一咖，一土一洋，两种大相径庭的品饮方式，已成为当下普洱人的时尚生活，也成为当下游客的打卡地。

美食也为茶乡普洱增添了不少魅力。这里有一种美食叫磨黑烧烤，烤猪蹄、烤鸡脚、烤韭菜、烤竹虫……应有尽有。不仅烤出了味道，也烤出了多少人难忘的美食回忆。

---

① 资料来源：云南普洱：景迈山冬日云海. 程浩，虎遵会. 人民网·云南频道，"学习强国"，2020年01月07日，摘自2022年6月25日。
在普洱，有一种美食叫磨黑烧烤. 董建华. 云南学习平台，"学习强国"，2020年01月19日，摘自2022年06月25日。
来云南吃一碗普洱镇沅县的"干板菜". 李飞雷. 云南学习平台，"学习强国"，2020年10月19日，摘自2022年6月25日。

还有一种美食，它外表不养眼，但与腊肉、香肠等食材搭配在一起便别有一番风味，这便是普洱镇沅县家喻户晓的秋藏美食——干板菜。干板菜的制作过程比较简单，制作原料是农家地头的青菜或大白菜。如今，随着生活水平的不断提高，干板菜也许并不具有多少吸引力，但到这里来一碗干板菜，会唤起你在鲜蔬甚少年代的乡愁记忆，从而更加珍惜现在的美好生活。也许这就是藏在美食中的人生感悟。

Section Four　　The Tea Town—Pu'er

Speaking of Pu'er, Yunnan, Pu'er tea is what has to be talked about first. And anyone who visit here, one of the major planting area of Pu'er tea, will taste it, feeling the time-endowed gift.

China is the country where tea was discovered earliest and drunk first. In China, there are many varieties of tea, but only Pu'er tea has become world famous despite its small planting land, and is considered the source of tea in the world. Only superior nature condition and time make the superior Pu'er tea. Depending on different processing techniques, there are two kinds of Pu'er tea— the raw Pu'er tea not processed by fermenting, and the cooked Pu'er tea processed by fermenting. In 2008, the processing technique of Pu'er tea, specifically, that of "Royal Tea" (the Tribute tea to imperial court) and Dayi Pu'er tea were selected in the National Intangible Cultural Heritage list. Tasting Pu'er tea is a process of appreciating the beautiful mountains and rivers in Yunnan, its distinctive culture and unique flavors. The Jingmai Mountain located in Pu'er, one of China's six tea mountains, is where the world-famous Ancient Tree tea is born. In winter there, tourists can see the beautiful sunset and sea of clouds while tasting Ancient Tree tea, which is a hard but very blessing encounter.

Pu'er is not only the home to tea, but also the nature-endowed planting land for coffee. Today, the city of Pu'er has become the largest area of planting coffee with the highest yield and the superior quality, and also the pivotal coffee trade center in China. One tea and one coffee, one is traditional, and the other is modern, two sharply different styles, but is the real picture of the modern Pu'er people's stylish life, and certainly the destination for tourists.

Apart from Pu'er tea, tasteful food is part of charming Pu'er. The first that must be mentioned here is Mohei barbecue with rich varieties of barbecuing pork trotters, chicken feet, leek, bamboo worms and so on. For its unique delicious taste, the delicacy brings back people's unforgettable memory of tasteful food.

One more delicacy that must be talked about is air-dried green vegetable or Chinese cabbage (the local calling is "Ganban vegetable"), which is plain in appearance but tastes good when cooked with preserved pork and sausages, thus becoming the household delicious food in autumn for the people in Zhenyuan county, Pu'er. It's simple to cook, because its material is common green vegetable and Chinese cabbage for every local family. Today, with people's life improving a lot, Ganban vegetable may have lost its glamour on the table, while having it may surely arouse your homesickness memory of those hard days with scarce green vegetable, and your awareness of cherishing the present happy life, which is something special about life we can feel by tasting delicacies.

第五节　侨乡腾冲[①]

　　位于中国西南边陲的云南省腾冲市与缅甸山水相连，是中国陆路通向南亚、东南亚的重要门户。依托这条古道，腾冲贸易兴盛，成为中国西南史上最古老的商埠。长期的开发、开放使腾冲成为全国著名的侨乡，处于边缘却不封闭，注重传承却不保守，深藏着浓厚的侨乡文化底蕴。

　　这里是中国第一魅力名镇和顺古镇的所在地，用"书香名里"形容和顺古镇再合适不过。这里有疏疏落落的古祠堂、古建筑和寺观；这里坐落着我国现存历史最悠久、最大的乡村图书馆和顺图书馆；还有历史上出了8个举人、403个秀才的文昌宫。景，文，境在这座古镇融为一体。

　　大自然赋予腾冲的还有火山地热资源。90多座休眠火山与周围的湖、泉、瀑布等丰富的景观，共同构成了我国规模最大的休眠期天然火山博物馆。火山运动造就的不同温度的暗河、温泉、喷井、瀑布等地热景观带给游人云深不知处的诗一般的仙境。1639年徐霞客的足迹留在了这里，如今循着他走过的痕迹，游人们重温并见证着他那描写地热景观的精彩文字。你也许无法清晰地记得这些文字，但一定会有自己的独特收获与感受。

　　腾冲市城郊随处可见各色荷花争奇斗艳，各种鸟儿在荷花丛中不时停留、嬉戏，荷香飘飘，鸟鸣啁啾，一副"鸟语荷香"的生态画卷，让人漫步其间，流连忘返。

[①] 资料来源：云南·和顺古镇. 赵庆祝. 云南学习平台，"学习强国"，2021年04月08日，摘自2022年07月02日。
　　腾冲掠影. 张海峰. 中国自然资源报，"学习强国"，2019年12月20日，摘自2022年07月02日。

Section Five   Tengchon—the Hometown of Overseas Chinese and Their Relatives

Tengchon, Yunnan, a city in the border of southwest of China, connected with Myanmar by mountains and rivers, is the primary way on land in China to South Asia and Southeast Asia. Depending on this, trade in Tengchon thrived and won Tengchon the oldest trading port in the southwest of China. For its long-term opening and development, Tengchon also became the hometown of overseas Chinese and their relatives. Amid opening and developing, the city attaches much importance to the impartment of its culture, which eventually contributes to its profound cultural deposits.

In Tengchon locates the first charming town of China—Heshun Town, which is riddled with scholarly and cultural atmosphere. Among the ancient temples, shrines and buildings scattered in order stands the biggest countryside library with the longest history—Heshun Library; here also stands Wenchang Palace, where in ancient time 8 scholars passed the imperial examination at the countryside level and 403 scholars passed the examination at the provincial level. Heshun Town is such a town endowed with fair scenery, thick cultural and scholarly atmosphere.

Tengchon is also endowed with natural volcanic and geothermal resources. More than 90 dormant volcanoes and its surrounding lakes, springs and waterfalls constitute rich landscapes, forming the biggest natural museum of dormant volcanoes. Movement of volcanoes brought about many hidden rivers, hot springs, gushy wells and waterfalls, which achieves a fairyland described in poem and gives tourists an illusion of being in the deep clouds, but can not tell where he is. In 1639, Xu Xiake, the famous geologist and traveller in Ming dynasty, left his footprints here. And now tourists, following his footprints, relearn and witness his amazing description of the geothermal landscape. Although you may have forgotten what he wrote, you will surely have your own experience and feeling here.

In every corner of the city, colorful lotus vie with each other to show their charm, attracting birds to rest among them, making fun, which forms a beautiful ecological picture with birds chirping among fragrant lotus. Walking there, you'll enjoy yourself so much that you just forget to leave.

> **Think and Discuss:**
> 1. 云南是一个你想发现美就能发现无数宝藏的神奇地方,你心中的云南是怎样的?
> 2. 文旅融合已经成为中国旅游发展的亮点。旅游集物质消费与精神享受于一体,旅游与文化密不可分。请从大学生的角度,以自己的家乡为例,谈谈如何打造更多体现文化内涵、人文精神的特色旅游。
> 3. 近日,号称"全国最美公路"的新疆独库公路却因旅游异常火爆,一度变为"垃圾公路""堵哭公路"。美丽的景色需要人们的共同守护,除了景区管理方的努力,还要靠游客们积极配合——文明旅游,从每一个细节做起。你认为如何才能提升游客的旅游素养?

参考文献
References

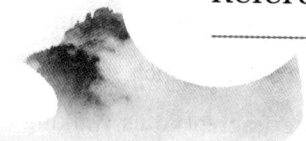

[1] 李孝友. 昆明风物志[M]. 昆明：云南民族出版社，1983.

[2] 王希信. 昆明都市文化研究[M]. 昆明：云南人民出版社，1999.

[3] 楚图南. 云南风物志[M]. 昆明：云南人民出版社，1986.

[4] 老楷. 老楷文、昆武画[M]. 昆明：云南人民出版社，2006.

[5] 云南信息报. 旧闻——昆明注事丛书[M]. 昆明：云南人民出版社，2009.

[6] 彭磊. 昆明六十年记忆[M]. 昆明：云南人民出版社，2010.

[7] 云南省历史研究所. 云南少数民族[M]. 昆明：云南人民出版社，1983.

[8] 云南省旅游局. 走遍彩云南[M]. 昆明：云南大学出版社，2010.

[9] 郭净，段玉明，杨福泉. 云南少数民族概览[M]. 昆明：云南人民出版社，1999.

[10] 张丹宇. 云南18怪[M]. 昆明：云南人民出版社，1999.

[11] 木丽春. 丽江古城史话[M]. 北京：民族出版社，1996.

[12] 和家修. 丽江民族文化建设探索[M]. 北京：作家出版社，2007.

[13] 李群育. 新编丽江风物志[M]. 昆明：云南人民出版社，2006.

[14] 李东红. 云南乡土文化丛书·大理[M]. 昆明：云南教育出版社，2000.

[15] 张锡禄，杨汝灿. 中国历史文化名城丛书·大理[M]. 北京：旅游教育出版社，2001.

[16] 合和. 细走云南·大理：风花雪月[M]. 昆明：云南大学出版社，2001.

[17] 赵寅松. 中国民族名片·大理白族[M]. 北京：民族出版社，2002.

[18] 《大理白族自治州概况》编写组. 大理白族自治州概况[M]. 北京：民族出版社，2007.

[19] 母锡鹏. 大理山水人文[M]. 昆明：云南民族出版社，2008.

[20] 彭国海. 谈天说地话大理[M]. 昆明：云南人民出版社，2009.

[21] 罗杨. 中国名城·云南大理[M]. 北京：知识产权出版社，2013.

[22] 杨定康，杨应康. 大理白族散记[M]. 昆明：云南民族出版社，2014.

[23] 《西双版纳傣族自治州概况》编写组. 西双版纳傣族自治州概况[M]. 北京：民族出版社，2008.

[24] 张俊著. 奇趣的西双版纳[M]. 昆明：云南教育出版社，2017.

[25] 百度百科. 西双版纳[EB/OL]. [2021-10-15]. https://baike.baidu.com/item.

[26] 360百科. 西双版纳热带雨林自然保护区[EB/OL]. [2021-10-17]. https:// upimg. baike. so.com/doc/8970111-9298287.html.

[27] 西双版纳新闻网. 从野象北迁看人象和谐[EB/OL]. (2021-06-15)[2021-10-20]. http://www.bndaily.com/c/2021-06-15/150837.shtml.

[28] 西双版纳傣族自治州人民政府门户网站. 中老铁路：奏响互利共赢最强音[EB/OL]. (2020-04-27)[2021-10-25]. https://www.xsbn.gov.cn/143.news.detail.dhtml?news_id=77367.

[29] 澎湃新闻客户端. 保护生物多样性，西双版纳在行动[EB/OL]. （2021-10-22）[2021-11-19]. https://m.thepaper.cn/baijiahao_15035352.

[30] 陈树华. 迪庆史话[M]. 昆明：云南人民出版社，2017.

[31] 合和. 迪庆香格里拉[M]. 昆明：云南大学出版社，2001.

[32] 勒安旺堆，史义，周国星. 香格里拉旅游指南[M]. 德宏:德宏民族出版社，1999.

[33] 约瑟夫·洛克. 发现梦中的香格里拉[M]. 冯媛，刘娟，译. 北京：北京理工大学出版社，2016.

[34] 马行云. 云南特色文化产业丛书——陶瓷卷[M]. 昆明：云南人民出版社，2015.

[35] 海男. 神性弥漫的行走：沿着香格里拉疆域的诗性笔记[M]. 昆明：云南人民出版社，2019.